W9-COW-078

Writing Was Everything

The William E. Massey Sr. Lectures
in the History of American Civilization
1994

ALFRED KAZIN

Writing

WAS

EVERYTHING

HARVARD UNIVERSITY PRESS

Cambridge, Massachusetts . London, England

1995

Copyright © 1995 by Alfred Kazin
All rights reserved
Printed in the United States of America

Library of Congress Cataloging-in-Publication Data

Kazin, Alfred
Writing was everything / Alfred Kazin.
    p. cm. — (William E. Massey Sr. lectures in the
history of American civilization ; 1994)
ISBN 0-674-96237-0 (alk. paper)
1. Kazin, Alfred, 1915–   . 2. American
literature—History and criticism—Theory, etc.
3. Criticism—United States—History—20th century.
4. United States—Intellectual life—20th century.
5. Critics—United States—Biography. I. Title.
II. Series.
PS29.K38A3 1995
809—dc20
[B]   95-6625

Designed by Gwen Frankfeldt

For Judith, of course

Contents

I was honored to be invited by the Program in the History of American Civilization at Harvard University to deliver the Massey Lectures. I am grateful to Professor Alan Heimert, Christine McFadden, and Dan Huesebosch for many kindnesses during my stay at Cambridge, and I owe a special debt to the doctoral students in American civilization who over several pleasant lunches educated me in their special concerns. My warmest thanks to old friends in the Harvard community—Daniel Aaron, William Alfred, and Monroe Engel come especially to mind—for their interest.

As usual, my wife Judith Dunford went over every word with her fine and unsparing critical intelligence. Many thanks to Aida Donald of Harvard University Press for her most friendly encouragement. My greatest debt is to my editor at the Press, Joyce Backman, who in her determined efforts to have me improve and connect the original lectures ignored my groans and managed to be charming and funny every step of the way.

A.K.
January 1995

prologue

All Critics Are Mortal

The reality of the *thing,* the return of the *thing.*
Structuralism and deconstruction . . . have
banished physical realities from literature,
replacing them with the abstract play of
language, the game of the signifiers. They were
on their way out anyway; they were leaving
literature; and the critical process, as usual,
found ways of explaining and rationalizing
their departure, even of suggesting they had
never been there.

—John Bayley, in *New York Review of Books*
  (June 4, 1981)

Y EARS AGO, when I was new to this curious business of being a critic and looked for guidance from my elders, I came upon two quotations in the same week that I dutifully wrote into my notebook. The first was from Goethe, who simply said, "Kill the dog, he's a reviewer!" The many composers, artists, and writers who like me have suffered and never forgotten a single line in a bad review still cheer Goethe on.

The second quotation was from Henry James, a busy reviewer in addition to being an unstoppably productive novelist, dramatist, and travel writer.

To lend himself, to project himself and steep himself, to feel and feel till he understands, and to understand so well that he can say, to have perception at the pitch of passion and expression as embracing as the air, to be infinitely curious and incorrigibly patient, and yet plastic and inflammable and determinable, stooping to conquer and yet serving to direct—these are fine chances for an active mind, chances to add the idea of independent beauty to the conception of success. Just in proportion as he is sentient and restless, just in proportion as he reacts and reciprocates and penetrates, is the critic a valuable instrument. (From *Essays in London and Elsewhere,* 1893)

Inspiring words, which James did not live up to. He could barely read poetry—he dismissed Walt Whitman's great opening poems on the Civil War—and tended to judge the novels of his day by his own example as a novelist. James was an incessant critic, but too much of a snob to respect as literary material any human experience he considered "low." He deprecated fiction that used dialect, and it is just as well that he paid no attention to the *Adventures of Huckleberry Finn*. He was so conscious of the Victorian moral tradition refuted and abandoned by the passionate novelists he reviewed, from Stendhal and Zola to Hardy and D. H. Lawrence—to say nothing of the lack of what he considered "form" in Tolstoy, whom he likened to an animal—that he raised prudence, in the form of pussyfooting and the art of malicious irony, to new heights.

The great critics have not been novelists but poets—Samuel Johnson, Wordsworth, Coleridge, Keats in his letters, Emerson, Baudelaire, Ezra Pound, T. S. Eliot—whose criticism sought to change the direction of literature so that people could read their poetry in the new spirit demanded of them. Tolstoy was a great novelist but such a moral universe unto himself that he came to suspect all art. In 1850 Melville the "isolato" (as he described himself and his heroes), in the rapture of discovering a kindred spirit in Nathaniel Hawthorne, said that "genius, all over the world, stands hand in hand, and one shock of recognition runs the whole circle round." Edmund Wilson, in the splendid 1943 anthology he called *The Shock of Recognition,* meant it to record the development of literature in the United States by the men who made it. But the only first-class critical intellect there to deal with his contemporaries was Edgar Allan Poe, who had wonderful instincts about work different from his own—and everything was. (In the end, though, he had the shrewdness of the paranoic about enemies who were real enough, since Poe antagonized everyone by his sense of superiority.)

What is so special in the criticism written by the creatively great is the inspiration they take from each other. Keats reading Shakespeare came to such self-recognition that he wrote in 1818, "Many have original minds who do not think it—they are led away by Custom . . . Now it appears to me that almost any Man may like the Spider spin from his own inwards his own airy Citadel . . . Man should not dispute or assert but whisper results to his neighbor." Turgenev, hailing Tolstoy as "Great Writer of the Russian Land," pleaded with him to give up his pose as a religious pilgrim and go back to writing fiction. Dostoevsky, at the dedication of the monument to Pushkin, reached such heights of rhetoric, in the way only Russians can in celebrating Pushkin, that long irreconciled enemies in the audience were moved to embrace one another. Nabokov so adored Pushkin that he insisted in his translation of *Eugene Onegin* on making the most literal possible version. Gorky said, in his poignant short memoir of Tolstoy in old age, "I am not an orphan on earth so long as that man exists." Thoreau told a friend that he had found in Emerson "a world where truths existed with the same perfection as the objects he studied in external nature, his ideals real and exact." Emerson, in his turn, wrote from Concord to Whitman in Brooklyn, July 1855: "I am not blind to the worth of the wonderful gift of *Leaves of Grass*. I find it the most extraordinary piece of wit and wisdom that America has yet contributed. I am very happy in reading it, as great power makes us happy . . . I give you joy of your free and brave thought . . . It has the best merits, namely, of fortifying and encouraging." And Emily Dickinson, in a letter: "We thank thee, Father, for these strange minds that enamor us against thee."

Now in all these fraternal tributes from the great to the great, there is a noticeable omission. No one is telling anybody exactly how to read a particular text; no one is warning anybody to discount as fallacious, ignorant, sexist, or politically dangerous someone else's reading. Keats, Turgenev, Emerson, and Thoreau are not professional critics—that is, people whose function is to tell other people How To Read, which naturally will include directions on what to look for in a text that other professional critics have missed.

For many years now, academics high and low have preempted serious criticism, have been riding herd on students who are so unused to general reading that they have little taste of their own and are glad to be told how to read, especially what to discount. This will get them closer and closer to the work of art. What nonsense. What gets us closer to a work of art is not instruction but another work of art. Only a plurality of choices can open up the new *thinking* in a work of literature that excites and liberates us. The poet Rilke said that "works of art are of an infinite loneliness, and nothing so little as criticism can reach them." What is of use to us in criticism is the *mind* of the critic. As Randall Jarrell once noted, some critics have the influence on young married couples that liberal clergymen used to have. Lionel Trilling was so compelling that he mesmerized many of his Columbia students for life, away from what he regarded as the illusions about progress fostered by the liberal imagination.

By contrast with such minds, in the 1930s the influence of Marxism-Leninism on the usual run of conformists was such that my students refused to read H. G. Wells because he was a bourgeois liberal. At a Modern Language Association convention in 1989—the session was called "The Muse of Masturbation," and it was thronged—it was noted that the hidden strategy of Emily Dickinson's poetry is in her use of "encoded images of clitoral masturbation to transcend sex-role limitations imposed by the 19th century patriarchy." The basic idea was that Dickinson loaded her work with references to peas, crumbs, and flower buds in order to broadcast secret messages of forbidden onanistic delights to other female illuminati. "Why does she write in such short, explosive sentences?" the speaker asked. "The style is clitoral, as far as I'm concerned."

The professional critic cannot tell people how to read without being bossy about what to read. There is a good deal to be gained from a strongminded critic who forces you to follow his reasoning, if not his taste. When the feisty traditionalist Allen Tate came out for Emily Dickinson, setting her against a background of declining religious belief in New England, he was disapproving of the decline, even condescending about it in his hierarchical southern way. But he did understand the anxious suspension of belief that Dickinson was talking about *in* her poetry, and hence the tension that makes her glorious. And that's what true criticism is: the ability to state preferences, to make choices on the basis of what is said in the only way available to that particular writer to say it.

But this is difficult and rare. Edmund Wilson had such a fine-tuned literary instinct that he considered Dante a steadier, greater craftsman than Shakespeare. But he didn't have enough patience with Dante's theology to show how the craft worked on the basis of the vision. In his marvelous first book of criticism, *Axel's Castle* (1931), Wilson knew exactly what Proust was doing because he could make connections: "Not only do his hero and most of his other characters pass into mortal declines, but their world itself seems to be coming to an end." Wilson's timing was fortunate when he finished toiling through Proust's seven books (thirteen volumes) in his own immaculate French. It was 1932, the depression was on, and he knew what a society in decline was like. Similarly, he read the early published fragments of

Finnegans Wake with such meticulous care that, for all the ingenuity of Joyce's style, he recognized how essentially passive, conventional, and even domestic Joyce's values were.

But who was there in the first decades of the century to recognize that despite all Dreiser's clumsiness, despite Theodore Dreiser's very personality, one might say, *Sister Carrie* was a true work of art and *An American Tragedy* an even greater one? H. L. Mencken championed *Sister Carrie* because its brutal honesty about sex knocked to pieces the WASP tradition that allowed Professor Charles Eliot Norton to warn Edith Wharton that no first-class work of fiction had ever been written about "illicit passion." Mencken was a German, he hated WASPs, and Dreiser was another German. But Mencken, as reactionary as Calvin Coolidge, could not tolerate the social truth of *An American Tragedy*.

It is all rather funny in a way. I have lived through the Marxist thirties, when Proust was consigned to the dustbin of history; and the New Criticism forties and fifties, when hungry sheep looking up to be fed found no Donne-like tension, paradox, or ambiguity in poor simple Walt Whitman; and the angry sixties, when I heard that William Faulkner contributed nothing to the civil-rights struggle; and the unfocused seventies and eighties and nineties, when the tides of ideology washed over me without mercy.

Living through all of this I have to say that, between racial-sexual-political partisanship and the devaluation of individual authorship by deconstructionists, criticism has become a threat to what my dear old teacher Mark Van Doren gallantly held up as the Private Reader.

Criticism as theory has so come to dominate the academy that Jonathan Culler at Cornell readily pronounces:

> Another way to put this would be to say that formerly the history of criticism was part of the history of literature (the story of changing conceptions of literature advanced by great writers), but that now the history of literature is part of the history of criticism. Specifically, the history of literature in our day depends on what happens in the critical communities in universities: what is canonized, what is explicated, what is articulated as a major problem for literature. (*Framing the Sign,* p. 40)

But that's not the whole problem. Nor is it just that so many people are angry. We live in a time that ominously foretells our future, and people are right to be dumbfounded by the thought. George Orwell immediately after the second world war, in an essay called "Why I Write," said that the writer's "subject matter will be determined by the age he lives in—at least this is true in tumultuous, revolutionary ages like our own—but before he ever begins to write he will have acquired an emotional attitude from which he will never completely escape."

The problem is that everybody has their reasons. No doubt this is what all the fratricide is about. But it so affects us that the common bond our culture once assumed no longer exists, when works of art conveyed an irremovable sense of the past (Faulkner said the past is not even past), and such was the central dimension of literature. We seem to forget that, just as theology takes the idea or the fantasy of immortality for granted, so literature seeks to reclaim the world that is constantly receding from us. The aim of literature has always been to reconcile us to life by showing that it is not limited to the actual data of existence. A real novel is harder to read than an essay in criticism, because the key to a work of imagination is the necessary relation of one part to another and of each part to the whole. Interpretation is generally loose, tries to make points. But criticism dominates when readers are insecure and easily impressed by any show of guidance. Only in an age so fragmented, so ignorant of the unlosable past working in us, can presumably literate persons speak of Dante, Beethoven, or Tolstoy as "dead white European males."

It is true that literature can no longer be regarded

anywhere as *the* truth about human existence, but then neither is science regarded like that. Despite the valiant claims—from Matthew Arnold to Wallace Stevens—made for poetry as a replacement for religion, nothing on that order of cosmic imagination has taken place. Poetry is too often satisfied with technical perfection and verbal surprise and, the early modernists aside, has little to say that requires so intricate a form of thinking as poetry. It is true, all too true, that literature is besieged by movies and hijacked by television, so commercialized that the million-dollar advances handed out to macho spy novelists makes life difficult for quieter talents. But is it necessary to value literature too by all that high-minded rage, to leave no quiet spot on earth for us to rejoin ourselves by reading, as it were? We have to remember our common humanity, leaving our much-needed liberations aside for the moment, and to realize that what drives the writer on is the radical insufficiency of language.

This does not mean that language is suspect in itself. Of course language is not the god that the romantics proclaimed. But what makes us uneasy is not what language does or doesn't do, but how it betrays the human heart. Language does not lie, brutalize, distort, exaggerate, evade, or kill; we do. When I despair of how little literature in our time expresses the shrinking of hope, the end of more than our century itself, I will go back to a certain passage from chapter 12 in *Madame Bovary* (in Francis Steegmuller's translation). After many weeks of lovemaking, the cold and shallow libertine Rodolphe is growing tired of Emma's passionate protestations of love:

> Since he had heard those same words uttered by loose women or prostitutes, he had little belief in their sincerity when he heard them now: the more flowery a person's speech, he thought, the more suspect the feelings, or lack of feelings, it concealed. Whereas the truth is that fullness of soul can sometimes overflow in utter vapidity of language, for none of us can ever express the exact measure of his needs or his thoughts or his sorrows; and human speech is like a cracked kettle on which we tap crude rhythms for bears to dance to, while we long to make music that will melt the stars.

chapter 1

Before the War

How intensely people used to feel,
like metal poured out at the end
of a proletarian novel.

—James Merrill, *A Different Person* (1993)

SIXTY YEARS AGO in the summer of 1934, nineteen years old and with a year to go at City College of New York, I became one of the crowd of hacks barely surviving the depression by doing book reviews for *The New Republic*. It was good luck, since I wasn't much interested in anything except reading and reporting in my notebook the direct impact of everything I read. Book and notebook went hand in hand. Valery Larbaud called a collection of his essays *Ce vice impuni, la lecture*—this unpunished vice, reading. For a long time, I am sorry to say, it was my only vice. But it led to my writing for a living. As a student I earned my keep by rewriting my dentist's literal English translation of his terrible Yiddish novel about the monotheistic pharaoh, Ikhnaton. I wrote term papers for the only rich boy at City College. I read to a blind classmate who, in the typical brutality of the time, had been left by his family to the mercies of the city, which paid me to read aloud for an honors thesis William Godwin's *Enquiry Concerning Political Justice* (considered radical in 1793).

As the whale-ship was for Herman Melville, reviewing was to be "my Yale College and my Harvard." Nothing really qualified me to write reviews at all, except that I was qualified for nothing else and for years had brooded in my notebooks trying to explain the hold of books on me. Once I graduated from *The Count of Monte Christo* to stray lines by Blake and Keats in Palgrave's *Golden Treasury,* I had to face the opening of *Crime and Punishment,* with Raskolnikov walking into the stench and madness of Petersburg's Haymarket, and the moodiness of Eugene O'Neill's early plays of the sea.

My pivotal experience of the raw hurting power that a book could have over me came when I first read *Oliver Twist.* I was twelve years old, sick with a fever in my narrow little bedroom, and frightened of the book as soon as Oliver fell into the hands of Fagin and his gang. But as I read on, I realized that in Dickens there are happy chapters in the country, among the rich, for all the cruel, scary chapters in London's dark underworld: city and country, dark and light, hell and heaven, cruelty and benevolence, destitution followed by lots of sunshiny moneyed comfort, a happy escape followed by recapture. Then Fagin, whom Dickens was always calling "the Jew," with his lisp and evil grin, would address the helpless Oliver with sinister sweetness as "My dear!" and once again frighten me as he frightened Oliver. In the end, though, everything is made right. Bill Sikes kills the pathetic Nancy for informing but, trying to escape the law, hangs himself in his own noose. The Jew in prison uselessly howls for his life. Justice is done, and Oliver comes into his rightful inheritance. All was well and would continue to be well, until Dickens came around in his next book with more bad news.

It became clear to me that Dickens had a bitterly intimate experience of social cruelty, and the name of that cruelty was England. He had to cheer up the reader and himself by coming up with the providentially rich and benevolent Mr. Brownlow, the sweet Mrs. Maylie and her protegée Rose. But they provided no relief from the hard and dark part. I didn't know Jews like Fagin. I didn't expect that anyone could think of a Jew as a master criminal instructing the young in crime. But what got to me most was Dickens' relentlessness in telling his story. He had put me in his power for life. Never before had I encountered in books such wild laughter or breakneck pace or insolence of mind. Dickens could barely contain his fury at the misery of England's abandoned failures and outcasts, the smiling heartlessness of the English class system. When I finally got to England during the war, *the* war of my generation, I understood all too well when I heard a Labour official say, "Dickens, not Marx, made socialists of us." But even as a boy I felt I was in Dickens' head and could not get out.

There was nothing to look at from my bed but a thin strip of wall next to the window, which opened on a fire escape. I was so shaken and seized by *Oliver Twist* that even when I put the book down I could see it going on, figure by figure, line by line, on the wall itself. Confined as I felt by my narrow room, by my bed, by fever, I felt a strange if awful happiness. *Oliver Twist* was all around me and in me. I wanted never to get away from its effect. There was something in this I had to track down: why was Dickens compelled to write like that, and why did it work on me like a drug? Since that was the literary problem I represented to myself, I had to figure it out for myself. That was how I started as a critic.

In 1934 the Great Depression—and the dream of revolution—was visible even at *The New Republic*. The magazine was famous for its association with John Dewey, Walter Lippmann, Randolph Bourne, and Van Wyck Brooks, famous for championing problematic modern writers—Edmund Wilson had been succeeded as book editor by the fellow-traveling Malcolm Cowley—and still occupied the old brownstone on West 21st Street where it had started in 1914. But Cowley was more accessible than Wilson, and the magazine was now besieged by starving reviewers begging for assignments.

I was awed by the history of the magazine (once supposed to reflect Woodrow Wilson's progressive views) and, as an instinctive partisan of the left, was still impressed by the successive emancipators of American life who had tramped through its pages. I valued even more highly its literary side, with the publication of such shocking new plainspeakers in poetry as Robert Frost. When Frost returned home from England in 1914 because of the war (he went there in 1912 to find a friendlier literary climate than late Victorian America), he was startled to find on the pier an early issue of the new magazine, which contained Amy Lowell's heartening review of his *North of Boston.*

Under Edmund Wilson's sporadic tenure and Malcolm Cowley's longer stay—Cowley was also a trenchant critic and a moving poet—*The New Republic* was crucial in encouraging and protecting supposedly unreadable and unacceptable modernists in literature. *Axel's Castle,* Wilson's epoch-making introduction to Yeats, Valéry, Eliot, Proust, Joyce, and Gertrude Stein, was serialized right in the middle of the journal, not at "the back of the book" usually consigned to mere literature. The same central place was also given to selections from Wilson's decisive and influential reporting in *The American Jitters: A Year of the Slump* (1932) and later to his study of the intellectual making of the Russian revolution, *To The Finland Station* (1940).

Axel's Castle was as important to me for its literary grace as for the news it gave me at seventeen of Joyce and Proust. To get the full effect of the lines with which Wilson ended his chapter on Proust, you had to be poor, a radical of sorts, and above all amazed to find a critic who could write like this:

> Proust is perhaps the last great historian of the loves, the society, the intelligence, the diplomacy, the literature and the art of the Heartbreak House of capitalist culture; and the little man with the sad appealing voice, the metaphysician's mind, the Saracen's beak, the ill-fitting dress-shirt and the great eyes that seem to see all about him like the many-faceted eyes of a fly, dominates the scene and plays host in the mansion where he is not long to be master.

The Communist critic Granville Hicks wondered if Proust would be read after the Revolution. Proust survived the revolution-that-never-happened as most so-called revolutionary writers did not. But this would-be elegy on Proust gives some idea of the socialist society that even so intellectual a man as

Edmund Wilson expected to replace the Heartbreak House of capitalism.

Wilson was as sedately arrogant as he looked (he once boasted to me that he often rewrote in his sleep the book he had just been reading), and was so eccentric and self-willed that his oddities alone made him a legend. In later life, disliking his passport photograph, he added whiskers to it. He took ideas, especially his own, with deadly seriousness, but he was far from being an original, systematic, or even consistent thinker. His convictions were unbelievably obstinate, especially when they reflected his disillusionment with ideals he once held. After decades of working on *Patriotic Gore,* his own Plutarchian history of Civil War personalities north and south, his bitterness in the 1960s about the general state of the country then led him to write a tortured introduction condemning Lincoln as another Lenin. This got rid of two old heroes at once but, as Bruce Catton said, showed that Wilson knew everything about the Civil War except why it was fought.

Wilson was not in the company of those poet-critics, from Wordsworth to Eliot, who changed the direction of literary thinking by their need to create a receptive audience for their creative work. He defiantly called himself a journalist, but more than most professors he was a relentlessly equipped scholar. Once he boasted to me that learning a new language (at the moment it was Hungarian) was like beginning a love affair. His honesty and thoroughness in mastering a new text, especially in a foreign language, thrilled me by its exigency. His favorite image was that of the critic as a watchmaker sharpening his lens. He had a particular gift for putting a writer into historical perspective, inserting the writer with his book into some great historical drama— such as the road from Michelet through Marx that ended with Lenin's arrival at the Finland Station in Petrograd to proclaim the establishment of the socialist order.

He was a teacher, a personal example, and I owe him much for showing me how to put a great writer solidly into one's consciousness. And what Wilson in the 1930s believed about the breakdown of American capitalism and the liberal tradition was also shared by the new writers for *The New Republic,* especially by me. I have never recovered from the thirties or wanted to. A son of the immigrant working class whose parents were tortured by poverty, I hardly needed the depression to be suspicious of moneyed power, or to see that in this society money is the first measure of all things and the only measure of many—or to learn for myself that there is no way in America of being honorably poor. Of course I couldn't know then that one day money would become the main interest of leading novelists whose agents, boasting of million-dollar advances, would display them like rock stars.

I was lucky to start out when I did. In those days you didn't have to be a professor—with a school, a line, a crowd of baby critics to proclaim your importance—in order to write serious criticism. Chancy as it was to depend for your bread on editors, many of whom took themselves more seriously than any mere writer ever could, I was happy to free-lance. My hero-critics were Wilson, Van Wyck Brooks, Randolph Bourne, Lewis Mumford, H. L. Mencken, George Bernard Shaw, G. K. Chesterton, Virginia Woolf in *The Common Reader*. Bliss it was in that new dawn to be a literary radical (mostly *literary*). To be young then was just the right time for fighting what in the universities was still the genteel tradition, when every real tradition in bankrupt America seemed to be falling down around us.

Many of the new contributors to *The New Republic* were so young that the editors once threw a party for those of us under twenty-five. In that summer of 1934, the bottom summer when the first wild wave of hope under the New Deal had receded and labor in San Francisco was calling a general strike, there were just too many of us wedged onto the single bench in the waiting room downstairs. We waited for Malcolm Cowley, handsome and as coolly macho as Clark Gable in his vivid seersucker suit, to sail in after lunch. There were so many more of us than he needed for reviews that Cowley, not knowing what else to do for the hungry bodies lined up to see him, would sell the books there was no space to review and dole out the proceeds to oldtimers and refugees, the more desperate cases haunting him for assignments. This didn't help the smoothly cultivated Englishman, an Oxford graduate, who used to sit next to me on the "hunger bench." He had no doubt come to God's country with dreams of a better life and was overwhelmed by America's depression. Only long after he disappeared from the bench did I hear that he had committed suicide, in a most literary way. He methodically starved himself to death.

The rage against capitalism was everywhere among writers and intellectuals, even in the South, the most feudal part of the country and the poorest, where half the farmers were tenants. The general pinch of depression made white planters exploit their black tenants more intensely than ever. There were over a hundred lynchings a year (these were just the ones reported). For both top and bottom people in the South, the Civil War had never really ended. The social bitterness and mutual suspicion between classes was the basic material that led William Faulkner back to the primitive foundations of southern society. He was galvanized by the image of one frontier succeeding another, one state of society after another, from the Appalachians to the Delta. Faulkner was scorned as a failure, called "Count No-Account" in his hometown of Oxford, Mississippi. But his integral vision of the South's eternal hatreds led him to write his greatest novels in this period—*The Sound and the Fury* (1929), *As I Lay Dying* (1930), *Light in August* (1932), *Absalom, Absalom!* (1936), *The Wild Palms* (1939), and *The Hamlet* (1940).

Faulkner did not idealize the South, like the deeply conservative southerners who issued their anti-industrial manifesto, *I'll Take My Stand,* in 1930. The agrarians never for a moment thought of blacks as fellow human beings. Faulkner, like most southerners of his class, had only banalities to offer on civil and human rights. But as an artist he transcends everyone, black or white, in his creation of Joe Christmas in *Light in August,* the racial outsider, the Christ-man open to everyone's hatred, and Dilsey in *The Sound and the Fury,* still bound to the aristocratic, degenerate Compsons, a human being presented to us as formed entirely by a lifetime of toil and sacrifice:

> She wore a stiff black hat perched upon her turban, and a maroon velvet cape with a border of mangy and anonymous fur above a dress of purple silk . . . She had been a big woman once but now

her skeleton rose, draped loosely in unpadded skin that tightened again upon a paunch almost dropsical, as though muscle and tissue had been courage or fortitude which the days or the years had consumed until only the indomitable skeleton was left rising like a ruin or a landmark above the somnolent and impervious guts . . .

But, still, there was an absolutism about *I'll Take My Stand* that brings back the outrage rankling everywhere in the thirties:

The theory of agrarianism is that the culture of the soil is the best and most sensitive of vocations, and that therefore it should have the economic preference and enlist the maximum number of workers . . . If a community, or a section, or a race, or an age, is groaning under industrialism and well aware that it is an evil dispensation, it must find the way to throw it off. To think that this cannot be done is pusillanimous. And if the whole community, section, race, or age thinks it cannot be done, then it has simply lost its political genius and doomed itself to impotence . . . The South needs orientation and direction in its thinking, and all things must begin at the point where it was thrown from its balance. It must know that the things for which it stood were reasonable and sound, that its condemnation at the hands of the North has been contemptible, and that for it, at

least, the philosophy of the North is the religion
of an alien God.

The language was rhetorical, inflamed by obstinate Confederate loyalties, and marked by a certain
aspiration to religious sensibility characteristic of
southern conservatives—some of whom still viewed
with equanimity the system that kept black people
in bondage and even branded some of them like
cattle. These literary claimants to Thomas Jefferson's
idealization of yeoman society were not too well
acquainted with the actual state of agriculture in the
South. I don't know whether the twelve writers who
took their stand—John Crowe Ransom, Allen Tate,
and Robert Penn Warren became the best known—
ever read the 1938 report to the president on economic conditions in the South by the National
Emergency Council. It said that over 60 percent of
the land in America most badly damaged by erosion
was in the southern states, that an expanse of southern farmland as big as South Carolina had been
gullied and washed away, that for generations thousands of southern farmers had plowed their furrows
up and down slopes so that each furrow served as a
ditch to hasten the runoff of silt-laden water after
every rain, and that malaria affected more than two
million people in the South.

In *After Strange Gods* (1934), lectures delivered

the year before at the University of Virginia, T. S. Eliot mirrored southern thinking about the "alien God" of the North when he said that "reasons of race and religion combine to make any large number of free-thinking Jews undesirable." I cite this not to complain sixty years after the fact about a statement Eliot is supposed to have retracted, or even to puzzle over the derision of Jews in his early work by someone who moves me more than any other twentieth-century American poet. No, antisemitism was a sign of these desperate days. You could fill up quite a shelf of modern literature just with writers who denounced or caricatured Jews in their work: Eliot, Pound, Hillaire Belloc, D. H. Lawrence, Louis-Ferdinand Céline, Wyndham Lewis. Even G. K. Chesterton, usually a most agreeable writer, in *The Everlasting Man* said that as part of their religion Jews do commit ritual murder. Hitler bound the masses to him by the violence of his hatred for Jews, and the extraordinarily gifted novelist Céline published antisemitic tracts, such as *Bagatelles pour un massacre,* which show how deeply and cruelly the crisis of the time ate into a writer already unhinged by his horror in the trenches of the first world war.

Despairing European intellectuals sought escapes in all directions. Even in the American South there were writers who longed for traditions that reached back to the Middle Ages. The conservatism behind

I'll Take My Stand eventually found its true outlet not in politics or social action, where the lowest white trash, the Snopeses, could outwit at every turn the gentry, the Compsons, Sartorises, and Faulkners, but in the New Criticism. Here a method of close reading replicated the *explication de texte* that many veterans of French classrooms remembered as an energetic teacher's surest way of making a student submit to authority, since the teacher always knew best what to extract from a given passage.

The New Critics claimed through the meticulous analysis of a poem to show just what poetry is. This kind of pedagogy, perhaps necessary at the time, given our hit-and-skip mass education, has clearly not fostered a love and feel for poetry as a wholly different *language,* as more than everyday language just adroitly elevated. And its image of poetry was hierarchical, usually fixed on the stuff that would meet T. S. Eliot's approval. The analysis of language could be gratefully received by undergraduates who by themselves would of course never recognize the cleverness of Andrew Marvell's "To His Coy Mistress," or who by themselves would be blind to all the metaphysical tension in John Donne's *Holy Sonnets,* the ambiguity, symbols, fused form, and post-Reformation disruption of the moral order. The idealization of poetry on the basis of the kind of poems the New Critics liked to analyze was bad enough. But when it came to fiction, the emphasis on intricate, allusive style completely cut out Defoe, Fielding, Dostoevsky, Zola, Dreiser, and other masters of forceful narrative.

Allen Tate was the best of the southern critics and the most intransigently reactionary. He was a gentleman-racist even when professing Catholicism; once he actually refused to shake hands with Langston Hughes. He used to entertain me on the summer sands at Wellfleet, where we regularly met in the sixties, by explaining that I would never "pass" if I wanted entrance to a certain southern ball, but that my blond wife had a chance. My only real contact with Tate was through music. We both played violin and would scratch our way enthusiastically through ancient duets while the philosophical Kenneth Burke, who knew a lot about music, would laugh at our mistakes.

Tate was not only a deeper writer than Warren or any of his other southern friends, but he really believed that the modern world was fallen, all fallen. The decay of the New England religious tradition was for him the most significant clue to the thinking of Emily Dickinson. Still, that certainly seems more to the point than the ideological delirium sweeping the 1990s, when we learn that the key to Emily Dickinson is clitoral masturbation.

CONTRARY TO THE BELIEF that the depression era saw nothing but proletarian literature, so haughtily disparaged as communist propaganda, the modernist fervor of the 1920s continued well into the 1930s and was still a passion with certain writers on the left. It was quite possible for a talented writer to follow the party line while despising its literary idiocy. Many of my friends belonged to the Communist Party or were close to it at one time or another, good and great writers such as Ignazio Silone, Romain Rolland, W. H. Auden, Stephen Spender, Bertolt Brecht, André Malraux, Graham Greene, Louis Aragon, Paul Eluard, Pablo Neruda, Theodore Dreiser (who died a member of the party), Ernest Hemingway, James T. Farrell, Lillian Hellman, and Henry Roth, whose *Call It Sleep* (1934) is the most authentic novel of the Jewish experience ever written by an American. The year 1934 also saw the publication of Farrell's first Studs Lonigan book and Hellman's *Children's Hour,* not to mention Robert Sherwood's *Petrified Forest* and Henry Miller's *Tropic of Cancer.*

At the same time, F. Scott Fitzgerald was telling his daughter at Vassar to read "the terrible chapter on the working day in *Das Kapital*" even as he was writing his exquisitely tragic and still underrated novel of marriage, *Tender Is the Night. Ash Wednesday,* that tormentedly beautiful and haunting stage in T. S. Eliot's struggle toward religious certainty, was published at the outset of the thirties by a poet who, as Hitler was proscribing the Jews, stated that if he were forced to choose between communism and fascism, he would lean toward fascism. (Later Eliot went on to deride some compassionate bishops in the Church of England who published a pamphlet on the sufferings of German Jews, and would himself become an icon for Sir Oswald Mosley's Union of British Fascists.)

Katherine Anne Porter's best work, the accomplished stories in *Flowering Judas,* in *Noon Wine,* in *Pale Horse, Pale Rider,* was published in the thirties, a time when the whole world was shaken by the ominous emergence of Nazism. She observed this for herself in miniature, as a moral breakdown among German passengers on the freighter *Vera* during a month-long voyage she took from Santa Cruz to Bremen. This experience, in 1931, so dominated her mind that she struggled for decades to turn it into an allegorical novel of the human condition—an arduous form for a writer schooled in the short story.

Her *Ship of Fools* did not appear until 1966. By then Porter's foreboding sense of political evil on the eve of Hitler's rise to power had turned into an acrid disillusionment with the human species and a flat belief that evil is always done in collusion with the good. I met Porter at Yaddo, the writers' colony in upper New York state, as she was writing her novel. She was a beautiful woman and in Hollywood's early days had actually been a bathing beauty for Mack Sennett. By the time I got to play poker with her and Carson McCullers one Sunday afternoon and to accompany her down Saratoga's Union Avenue—Henry James once called it the most beautiful street in America—she had become a terrible hater. She had malicious things to say about every girl we passed on our walk, contemptuously dismissed my admiration for D. H. Lawrence, and would have gone on with the same spite about Carson McCullers if I had not objected.

The left-wing novelist Josephine Herbst—the second book in her 1930s trilogy was called *The Executioner Waits*—was one of Katherine Anne's closest friends. They wrote to each other all the time. This did not stop Porter from reporting her friend to the FBI during the war, which cost Herbst a desperately needed job with the government's information services. I was not surprised in later years to learn that Porter's private papers contained obscene racial epithets for James Baldwin and sneers for Saul Bellow (Jews, she said, didn't have the background to use the English language properly).

Violence of feeling marked the thirties in every

sphere, not least among the righteous. In 1933 I angrily walked out of a synagogue when I heard the rabbi intone that Hitler was God's punishment for our sins. The right saw Hitler as another instance of a treacherous, flowering-Judas that had been falling since the Middle Ages, or perhaps just since the French revolution. The left declaimed against a fallen society. Yet Henry Roth's *Call It Sleep* was inspired by Joyce's use of stream-of-consciousness as the true language of the human heart. The book belongs to the considerable side of the 1930s that still held literature sacred.

Call It Sleep was condemned by the Communist *New Masses*—which no doubt expected another proletarian novel like Michael Gold's *Jews Without Money*—as "introspective and febrile," lacking the required determination to change the world. The world did not welcome the book until it was reissued in 1964, when it had an international success. What made the book last is Roth's determined sense that art invents truth better than any document can. A special idiom is required to render little David Schearl's entrance into the hostilities of New York. He is so deeply attached to his mother and she to him that Yiddish—her only language—has become as exclusive as their relationship to each other. David's father wants to believe that the boy is not his son and is hateful to them both, which reinforces David's tie not only to his mother but to her Yiddish. A second language is spoken in the street outside this riven family, a guttural, distorted English that David has to learn at the risk of adopting the street's brutish values.

In the end, only a third language gives meaning to the boy's existence, a masterly English founded on the senses, fresh and independent, culminating in the personal rhythms, images, and dreaming mental world that Roth learned from Joyce:

The silent white street waited for him, snow-drifts where the curb was. Footfalls silent. Before the houses, the newly swept areas of the sidewalks, black, were greying again. Flakes cold on cheek, quickening. Narrow-eyed, he peered up. Black overhead the flakes were, black till they sank beneath a housetop. Then suddenly white. Why? A flake settled on his eye-lash; he blinked, tearing with the wet chill, lowered his head. Snow trodden down by passing feet into crude, slippery scales. The railings before basements gliding back beside him, white pipes of snow upon them. He scooped one up as he went. Icy, setting the blood tingling, it gathered before the plow of his palm . . . Voices of children. School a little way off, on the other side of the street . . . Must cross. Before

him at the corner, children were crossing a beaten
path in the snow. Beside him, the untrodden white
of the gutter.

To dwell like this on each speck of one's innermost
sense of being is to be alone, outside the safety net
of Jewishness. This "kid"—there is a Christ-like kid
motif in the book—must do the unbelievable thing.
So at the end he shocks himself into unconsciousness by inserting the metal dipper of a milk can into
the trolley tracks: "Between the livid jaws of the rail,
the dipper twisted and bounced, consumed in roar-
ing radiance, candescent." David is after epiphany,
the radiant power ("strangest triumph, strangest ac-
quiescence") that Henry Roth finds only in writing
Call It Sleep. His second novel would not appear for
sixty years, the beginning of his massive, drawn-out
Mercy of a Rude Stream.

THE SO-CALLED minority writers of the 1930s
blazed up for a season and then either gave up
or, like Richard Wright, went into exile—not least
from the American black community, who usually
didn't read him and, if they did, wouldn't take him
seriously as an artist.

Wright was born in Mississippi in 1908 and died
in Paris in 1960, only fifty-two. I regard him as the

strongest and most enduring black talent in twentieth-century American writing. He had a total grievance about life in America—you might say he was
born into it as well as with it—which took him into
the Communist Party through the John Reed Club,
set up as an association of writers for just this purpose.

In 1950 *The God That Failed* came out, a collection
of essays about their relationship to the Communist
Party by six writers: Wright, Arthur Koestler, Ignazio
Silone, André Gide, the journalist Louis Fischer, and
Stephen Spender. Wright remembers that in the John
Reed Club, "I was meeting men and women whom
I should know for decades to come, who were to
form the first sustained relationships of my life." But
in the party "I was suspected because I wanted to
reveal the vast spiritual and physical ravages of Negro life, the profundity latent in these rejected people
. . . What was the danger in showing the kinship
between the sufferings of the Negro and the sufferings of other people?" Later a black man calls him a
"petty-bourgeois degenerate," and he gets beaten up
by whites as some blacks look on. "You lost people!"
he cries out, banging his fist on the table. He tries
to resign, is told that no one can resign from the
party, and is then expelled. Summing up his difficul-
ties: "I don't want to be organized . . . Nobody can
tell me how or what to write." Yet he never lost a

certain nostalgia for the communists he met in the club. They were, after all, the first to recognize him as a writer.

I knew Wright a little, occasionally had dinner with him at Frank's Restaurant in Harlem. He was handsome, restlessly eager, and, even when *Native Son* in 1940 astonishingly became a bestseller, unsatisfiable. Like many writers of the thirties who had grown up in the deepest poverty, Wright *looked* professionally angry. James T. Farrell was another such: he was swift to call his opponent in an argument "You phony!" and, though the most vulnerable of men, would strike a tough pose with a cigarette butt hanging from a corner of his mouth as if to warn you that he could get even tougher. Not for the likes of them was Edmund Wilson's praise of Hemingway for showing "grace under pressure"; that was in another country. Wright's country was Mississippi in the twenties, when he was stripped naked by his mother and badly beaten with a barrel stave because he had fought back against some white boys. He was slapped around by his grandmother, a fanatical Seventh Day Adventist, for repeating a story she called "Devil stuff in my house." After he retaliated with a cuss word, she beat him so hard that he was sure she would kill him if he didn't get out of her reach.

"I used to mull over the strange absence of real kindness in Negroes," Wright wrote in *Black Boy,* his extraordinary personal history of unrelieved oppression both in and out of the black community. This book becomes a distinctive literary accomplishment through Wright's most striking technical gift: his sense of momentum, his way of seeing life as act after act after act in an atmosphere of undeviating cruelty. The reader gets breathless sharing Wright's intensity.

Wright was not afraid to admit that he had more than a touch of cruelty himself. Once when his terrible father ordered his sons to get rid of a kitten, Wright and his brother hanged it as a way of doing the father one better. Killing is as routine in Wright's work as it is in Dostoevsky's. Dostoevsky used the act of murder to highlight all that was hidden in the seething, madly resentful Karamazovs or the unyielding Raskolnikov totally possessed by his own program. In Wright the race question is certainly not hidden. As with all black writers, it is the atmosphere he breathes, it is America. But his subject *is* the black condition—he does not celebrate blackness itself.

It was different back then: the 1930s forced an urgent, *direct* sense of social reality. To be black was to be confined to what Wright called "nothingness." He says at the beginning of *Native Son* that Bigger would have to kill himself or someone else if "he allowed what his life meant to enter fully into his consciousness." What makes Wright so remarkable an artist of his protagonist's unconsciousness is that the rage in Bigger becomes the wholly individualized drama of his break with the past, his falling into the ultimate act of murder, without ceasing to be an accusing representation of the one world Bigger knew.

Wright is able to make us see Bigger's violence and the white world's hostility even before he commits murder. Then the whole of Chicago unites to hunt him down. Bigger is a hopelessly sullen, twenty-year-old black man, constantly at odds with his family and his neighborhood pals, who is hired by wealthy liberals, the Daltons, as chauffeur and handyman. Mrs. Dalton is blind; Mr. Dalton, who gives generously to black causes, owns slum properties all over the city, like the one in which Bigger's family lives. Their daughter Mary is a do-gooder whose yearning to do something for the underprivileged takes the form of a romance with a white communist, Jan. Their attempts to recruit Bigger, at least intellectually, make him even more uneasy about these crazy white folk. Mary and Jan insist on Bigger's taking them to a black restaurant, and they get very drunk. Jan goes home, leaving a semiconscious Mary in Bigger's care.

He gets her to her room, is sexually stirred, but just then Mary's blind mother enters the room, a "white blur," so alarming him that he puts a pillow over Mary's face to keep her quiet, and smothers her to death. He forces the corpse into a trunk, gets it to the basement, and after whacking off Mary's head with a hatchet, thrusts the body into the blazing furnace. He writes a crude kidnap note to the family, calling himself a communist. He confesses to his terrified girlfriend Bessie but, after making love, batters her with a brick and throws the body down an air shaft. Over and over he reasons: "He could not take her with him and he could not leave her behind." Finally apprehended, with Chicago in convulsions of race hate over the crime against the white woman, he is defended by a communist lawyer who ridiculously tries to save him from the chair by reciting the full history of black oppression in the United States.

It is impossible to view Bigger's terrible acts—especially his murder of Bessie, who loves him and tolerates his using her because it's the only way of keeping him—as just another despairing reaction to white oppression. But Bigger is a character in a novel, not a case history, and he is a convincing character, unforgettable in all his sullenness, indifference, dumb misery, and violence, because he *acts,* acts all the time. For all the abstract idealism that goes into the defense lawyer's final plea to the jury—a speech that blacks today can't read without laughing—Wright was so habituated to violence every hour of his early life that to read the autobiographical *Black Boy* is to share his suffering. In the same way, I still can't read *Native Son* without feeling as confined as Bigger and wanting to burst out.

The crux is the deed, not the justification or interpretation of the deed, which is always secondary no matter how brilliant. The rest is what follows necessarily from that first irrevocable action. Bigger thinks: "In all of his life these two murders were the most meaningful things that had ever happened to him. He was living, truly and deeply." The centrality of some great and usually dire action that decides the future—Eve succumbing to the serpent, Cain killing Abel, Oedipus not knowing that it is his father he kills and his mother he marries—is the truth at the heart of literature. And it was a truth I learned to watch for in the cruel 1930s. It was in America that I learned of Hitler's Germany and Stalin's Russia. The South took center stage because everything descended for southerners, white or black, from the one historical act that in 1619 first brought black slaves to Virginia. Another Mississippian, William Faulkner, admired and encouraged Wright, but regretted his preoccupation with the black condition. Yet in Faulkner too we can never let that single drastic event go, for it would mean an end to all the human history lived in the experience and heritage of slavery.

I was not altogether ready for Faulkner when I reviewed *The Wild Palms* in 1939. My psychological state, and my old vice, was that of the bookish intellectual, the onlooker. In wartime I was to travel through the South as a reporter, observing chain gangs at work and black soldiers burned by lighted cigarettes in the hands of white soldiers. But in the earlier days I could recognize what I called Faulkner's special effort, "that wonderful and maddening lyricism that bursts out of his pages like fire, that gnawing obsession with his characters that shreds their nerves down to the last fiber." *The Wild Palms,* in surprisingly avant-garde manner, consisted of two stories printed simultaneously, a page from one followed by a page from the other. One story was about a young doctor and his mistress doomed by their inability to escape each other and, the second, about a convict, let out of jail to help build a dike against the flooding river, who finds himself free and doesn't want to be. I darted back and forth over the stories to explore what in my review of the book I called "the limitless spaces of the heart's weariness and abnegation":

> With Faulkner's sensitiveness to the innermost patterns of atmosphere, the slow, limited circle of these movements is expanded by its force. The world in which two death-loving people fall in love and torment each other across a dozen states

is illuminated by the shock of Faulkner's relentlessness—the pin-point details in the slope of a river, the twist of a tree in its soil, the surge of unuttered speech. Such intensity breaks the novel wide open, as Faulkner descends one step after another of his imagination to get at root ends, where sensations contract and expand like tropical flowers. Faulkner's power to elaborate a single scene has never been more dramatic—up to the clashing of the wild palms in the gardens of New Orleans and the days spent in Chicago hotels.

There is a relentlessness like this in *Native Son* when we get to the "white blur" in Mary's room as the blind mother enters. So Mary is suffocated and everything follows: the way Bigger doubles over Mary's legs to get her into the trunk, the trunk forced into the furnace, another white blur in the form of a cat, the furnace blazing like "an enraged beast." With Bessie, Bigger feels that he is "on some vast turning wheel that made him want to run faster and faster," and he sees Bessie's breath "as a white thread stretching out over a vast black gulf," which he clings to for life before lifting the brick again and again to bash her to death.

Native Son was a startling bestseller when it was published in 1940, and was even selected by the Book of the Month Club after Wright reluctantly agreed to cut certain sexual scenes and speeches to the jury by the prosecution and defense. Wright did reject a film offer for *Native Son* in which all the main characters would have to be white. (Years later, Wright himself starred as Bigger in a film made in Argentina.)

Wright has never been a favorite with black writers and intellectuals. He believed in renewing the American imagination with a directness that was too blunt about blacks, not only about the black condition, even for the 1930s. Wright's remarkable narrative gift was ignored, and his radicalism emptied of its subtlety, by James Baldwin in a supercilious 1949 essay, "Everybody's Protest Novel," where *Native Son* becomes as simple-minded as *Uncle Tom's Cabin*. (I don't believe that *Uncle Tom's Cabin* is simple-minded or that Uncle Tom was an uncle tom.) In another essay, "Many Thousands Gone" (1951), Baldwin charged Wright with treating racism as "a social and not a personal or human problem . . . somehow analogous to disease—cancer, perhaps, or tuberculosis, which must be checked even though it cannot be cured." Even more, "Wright had the necessity thrust on him of being the representative of some thirteen million people." Poor Wright could never live up to that; *Native Son* could not make the difference Wright was dreaming of.

But of course the more polished and sophisticated Baldwin thought *he* could. With the powerful rhetoric absorbed as a boy preacher in Harlem, Baldwin proclaimed that the underlying bond between oppressor and oppressed could not be released "until we accept how very much it contains of the force and anguish and terror of love." That should be good news for racists and bigots everywhere.

THE MOST INTERESTING young writer on the hunger bench at *The New Republic*—and a very short time did he sit there—was John Cheever. He was a favorite of Cowley's, and obviously slated for higher things than reviewing instantly forgettable novels in 150 words. In 1991, reading Cheever's published journals, so elegantly and acceptably scandalous by the tastes of the 1990s, I thought back to our first meeting around 1937.

The New Republic had moved itself uptown to smart-looking new offices at 40 East 49th, just off Madison. Cheever and I met at that memorable party for contributors under twenty-five. The magazine wanted to publicize all that youth. Cheever, who for some reason liked to sign his name "Jon" under his little reviews, published his first story in *The New Republic* at eighteen. It was about his expulsion from Thayer Academy in Massachusetts, the last educational institution he ever attended. He was going to

free-lance himself, in every sense, for the rest of his
life.

What I remember most about the party was
Cheever, short and slight, lithe as a jockey, moving
among the guests with a confident authority that
dazzled me. He was as deliciously quick in his movements as Fred Astaire. I was mesmerized by his
inborn social sense. Myself an awkward and resentful wallflower from darkest Brooklyn, where my
friends had no small talk and got together only to
chew each other up in radical political argument, I
could see that Cheever knew exactly what to say to
people he had just met, that he was witty as hell and
cheerfully expected his best sallies to be remembered. He was already somebody and on his way to
something big.

Years after the war, whenever I met up with him
at Yaddo or some literary gathering, Cheever seemed
astonishingly unchanged, as bubbly and social as
ever, charming people up and down, laughing as if
the party would never end and the lights would
never go out. By this time I had been reading him
for years and was taken by his talent, sultry and
lyrical at once, marked by a deadly distrust of the
suburban life he himself was living in Ossining (a
town also occupied by Sing Sing Prison). I considered him the most poignant, accomplished, and un-

predictable writer in *The New Yorker*'s very predictable fiction stable. What struck me in Cheever's stories was the personal suffering of characters firmly embedded within the most bourgeois of circumstances, which were quietly unsympathetic and, at worst, discreetly hostile. It didn't seem to matter that the always clever protagonist was internally dying in suburbia or that his melancholia had been advanced by too many martinis.

The style was verbally irreproachable too—"almost perfect," as the editor William Shawn liked to say about a story he particularly liked. Ever since the days of Harold Ross, its first editor, *The New Yorker* seemed focused on style in all things. In prose this meant what I came to call the sudden drop shot—the ability to insert a smartly unexpected word or turn around a sentence so that the reader would think, "Um, how well written, how clever!" Here is Cheever introducing his collected stories: "These stories seem at times to be stories of a long-lost world when the city of New York was still filled with a river light, when you heard the Benny Goodman quartets from a radio in the corner stationery store, and when almost everybody wore a hat." He wrote in this style and tradition as if he never had to learn it. Still the stories were wryly serious, desperately ironic, full of that special distrust of postwar American hedonism felt to the point of hysteria by those who had seen the depression end, but only with the war. And they were funny, in Cheever's politely macabre way, with the contrast between suburbia and the despair within, which sounded like a kind of mutiny against family life that could not hope to succeed.

Cheever in his polite hopelessness knew exactly the emotional tone he was writing from and aiming for. As he put it in the middle of one story, "Why, in this half-finished civilization, this most prosperous, equitable and accomplished world, should everyone seem so disappointed?" That, it not surprisingly turned out, was what his private journals were all about, and done with his usual cleverness and show of style.

In 1991 *The New Yorker*'s editor Robert Gottlieb estimated that he made selections for the published journals from what could have been four million words. Whatever remained in that vast abyss cast a shadow of despair on the smooth pages that were published. One felt and heard, despite Cheever's best professional style (parts of the journal read like yet another Cheever story in *The New Yorker*, and they were in fact serialized there), the curse that even the luckiest of mortals can't help shouting against life, at least once. Cheever was always in crisis, and it was a crisis never resolved in any of his stories, left hanging in the air after the story is done. His Episcopal churchgoing—the only grace in his life except writing, his one transcendental country, a ritual repair in a life lived day to day from trial to trial—did nothing to relieve his doubleness as a married man sexually involved with other men or as a drinker so committed that he drove his family crazy looking for bottles in expertly hidden places. Cheever's journals took me back to the debonair boy I had met at *The New Republic* during the depression. The society manner he kept through life had served him well. In his pages, literature and life are necessarily intimate. The one lesson as a critic I seem to have been born with is that no storyteller can escape that intimacy.

Literary journalism today is smarter, more detached, always performing and performative, than it was when I began. Everyone in those ancient days knew that writing criticism was the booby prize for people who were not creative—that is, all those who couldn't write novels. But as I broke into magazines and newspaper supplements in the thirties, I found reviewing exciting enough. These are some of the books I tackled on my own: Silone's *Fontamara,* Céline's *Death on the Installment Plan,* Thomas Mann's *Joseph in Egypt,* Faulkner's *The Unvanquished,* Sherwood Anderson's *Kit Brandon,* Ramon Sender's *Seven Red Sundays,* James T. Farrell's *No Star Is Lost* and *A World I Never Made,* Djuna Barnes's *Nightwood,* Hemingway's *To Have and Have Not* and *The Fifth*

Column and First Forty-Nine Stories, the New Directions anthologies, Christina Stead's *House of All Nations,* André Malraux's *Man's Hope,* Malcolm Cowley's anthology *After the Genteel Tradition,* Israel Joshua Singer's *East of Eden,* Edouard Dujardin's *We'll to the Woods No More* (1888, the first stream-of-consciousness novel), Roger Martin du Gard's *The Thibaults,* B. Traven's *The Bridge in the Jungle,* William Carlos Williams' impressive novel *White Mule,* Cyril Connolly's *Enemies of Promise,* George Bernanos' *Diary of a Country Priest,* Edna Millay's *Conversations at Midnight,* Thomas Wolfe's *The Web and the Rock,* Christopher Isherwood's *Goodbye to Berlin,* John Dos Passos' *Adventures of a Young Man.*

Because of my love of James Joyce, I even had the nerve to try a review of *Finnegans Wake* in 1939. I happened to be in the office of Harold Guinzberg, the head of Viking Press, when the first copy of the just-published *Finnegan* was placed on his desk. He was a very quiet, nice businessman who had previously manufactured baby things and dress shields. He seemed dazed, even frightened, by the sight of this thick black volume, which he obviously had no intention of opening. When I asked him how he happened to be publishing *Finnegans Wake,* he said helplessly, "Well, we asked Mr. Joyce for his next book. This seems to be his next book."

I was too young to have studied "Anna Livia

Plurabelle" and the other sections of Joyce's work in progress that came out long before 1939. But always captured by Joyce's lilting cadences, the finest music in twentieth-century prose—as a young socialist I would repeat softly "O Parnell, my dead king!" in tribute to Eugene V. Debs as I entered the Brownsville Labor Lyceum on Powell Street—I managed to work through a large chunk of the book, to hop and jump through the rest, and was astonished to read that mine was among the few reviews that Joyce could tolerate.

As I look over my piece, which appeared in the *Herald Tribune* book supplement on May 21, 1939, I can't see why Joyce liked it. But I am proud that in a period dominated and sometimes tyrannized by social concerns, my own not least, I responded so ardently to Joyce's invention of one man's unconscious in a language from below, the dream language that washes like a great wave across each page and still sends me overboard:

Ho hang! Hang ho! And the clash of our cries till we spring to be free. Auravoles, they says, never heed of your name! But I'm loothing them that's here and all I lothe. Loonely in me loneness. For all their faults, I am passing out. O bitter ending! I'll slip away before they're up. They'll never see. Nor know. Nor miss me. And it's old and old it's

sad and old it's sad and weary I go back to you,
my cold father, my cold mad father, my cold mad
feary father, till the near sight of the mere size of
him, the moyles and moyles of it, moananoaning,
makes me seasilt saltsick and I rush, my only, into
your arms. . . . So soft this morning, ours. Yes.
Carry me along, taddy, like you done through the
toy fair!

Ever since I surfaced at the end of *Finnegans Wake,*
blinded and drownded, as the old lady says in *A
Portrait of the Artist as a Young Man,* I repeat those
last lines like a prayer. In my review I noted that the
sleeping hero, Humphrey Chimpden Earwicker
(H.C.E., or Here Comes Everybody), is alone, but
when he isn't dreaming about himself, life spills out
in staggering profusion—a song turns into a
woman's face, an enemy grows devil's horns, Wel-
lington leans out of his statue. So I wrote: "It is as
if a God were looking at life not as a chapter in
history . . . but as something stupendous in its dis-
organization, a clutching of many hands, a blind and
mangled effort to rise from the slime, the great desire
to assume identity." And with this I added, sure that
it was a central drive of the book, "Joyce has made
of sleep an instrument of satire. Sleep not only re-
verses normal daily consciousness; it mocks it."

This power given to the self in sleep, like Proust's

remembrance of lying between sleep and waking at the beginning of *Swann's Way*, was prodigious for me, a revelation of strange horizons in words beyond words. In 1938, newly married at twenty-three and living on Remsen Street in Brooklyn Heights—my ideal New York neighborhood, with access to the harbor and the great Brooklyn Bridge—I began to keep a daily journal as I worked on my first book. I needed to note to myself all sorts of stray things, from my great happiness with my young wife, my infatuation with the literary America I was absorbing in all-day bouts of reading in the great central reading room, number 315, of the New York Public Library, and my intense experience of the streets and people interfused by the city of New York. From my journal, February 28, 1942:

> Every once in a while a sentence in a book is a voice heard, recalling for me the delight in American landscape that I felt as I began serious work on *On Native Grounds*. The sentence this morning, fresh as a spring wind, is from Constance Rourke's book on Audubon. His ornithology tokened the newly recognized national sense of scale. Like Whitman's lines, Audubon's birds spoke for a continent. Rourke recalls the excitement under which I lived for weeks and weeks early in 1939, when I recognized my professional as well as passionate interest in so much long-past American writing

and art. In those weeks I used to walk up and down the halls of the Metropolitan Museum's American galleries, delighted by the dull glazed views of a Sunday morning in 1836 in the village of Flatbush, the solemn faces of colonial and revolutionary worthies as they posed for history—how different from the struggle to express character in the work Thomas Eakins made of the human face!

These images brought back the delight I had always taken in documents of American history, in biographical accounts of Americans at all times and in all conditions. As a senior at City College, one of my jobs under the National Youth Administration was to comb the *Dictionary of American Biography* for the names of southerners who had graduated from college before the Civil War. I never tired of reading their stories. Continuing in my journal:

God, the pleasure I get from the methodical study in these years of American texts for my book. True, I get the deepest fulfillment only out of a few Americans. When I think of *writing,* I think first of Blake and Tolstoy. Yet the very words "poet of American nationality"—meaning those who created my sense of America—bring back the deepest individuality: William James, Benjamin Franklin, the isolates Albert Pinkham Ryder and Emily Dickinson. Lewis Mumford's *The Brown Decades* brought me to the deteriorating Ryders in the Brooklyn Museum and to the genius behind Brooklyn Bridge, John August Roebling, to the letters of William James, to Emerson's journals. Makers and movers and thinkers all. What adventuresomeness and purity taken together. What heroism and *salt*.

chapter 2

During the War

The real war will never get into the books.

—Walt Whitman, *Memoranda during the War* (1875)

I have something to report that lies beyond the imagination of mankind.

—London *Times* correspondent from Belsen (April 1945)

For the last seven months of the war, in 1945, I was in Britain on assignment to report on the social crisis that was increasingly revealing itself in the British armed services and the wartime factories. I had no sooner landed in Liverpool from my Liberty ship, incredibly named the S.S. *Hart Crane,* than I thought of Herman Melville arriving in the same port a century before. The bleak vista before me was what Melville had seen and described in *Redburn:* "Poverty, poverty, poverty in almost endless vistas; and want and woe staggered in arms along these miserable streets."

Going beyond the old bitterness about Britain's class distinctions and the neglect of public education, there was widespread anxiety about what everyone called "Civvy Street," the postwar civilian future. It turned morale sour. The famous unemployment of the thirties that had staggered even the Prince of Wales was still a terrible problem. Miles and miles of bombed houses remained unrestored.

The first postwar election, to the astonishment and outrage of Americans, ousted Winston Churchill. That victory of the Labour Party owed much to the rousingly critical and often intensely radical discussion groups during the war all over England, Wales, and Scotland—set up by the Army Bureau of Current Affairs. American forces would soon follow suit, but without the British sense of national crisis. It was my particular task to report on just this. Every phase of British society, every long-standing grievance, was discussed on army time as a routine part of military life. The program was conceived by the War Office in 1940 in response to near mutiny on the part of the defeated and exhausted troops who had crawled to Dunkirk, without military equipment and most of their personal possessions, only to be bombed by the Luftwaffe. Class privilege decided who would be the first to get picked up by the more splendid yachts sent out from England. Morale was so low afterward that the War Office declared (in a statement inconceivable to Americans), "We are going Left with the troops."

Many of the soldiers, sailors, and airmen I met, to say nothing of the traditionally Labour workers in the factories, gave me the impression that much of England had already gone left, sharply and bitterly so. The impression was one-sided. My super-English landlady in Great Cumberland Street (she was from

Virginia) had a husband, a major in the army, who pronounced himself disgusted by the "Labour johnnies" who were promising the workers a better England after the war. "This war is a revolution, is it? Not where we sit it isn't!"

To my partisan eyes, injustice to its own people kept England the seething social laboratory it had been in the nineteenth century—when the brutality of the factory system made it prime material for the propagation of Marxism. In the slums and along the docks, beautiful English children ("Non angli sed angeli," Pope Gregory had said in the sixth century when he saw some blond English captives) ran red-cheeked in the cold. Watching them I wondered if they would grow up to look like the scrawny, chalk-faced men with workers' caps and thin scarves who toiled in the maze of shadows along the docks, where hand-lettered signs had been put up reading "Hands Off Greece." At least the children were getting a ration of orange juice from the government. But I noticed in the behind-scenes talk of officers that what worried authorities most about the lower classes was not their spindly, grimy bodies and their "dirty feeding habits" but that the nation would be "seriously weakened" by so many damaged people. Even Tories were warning, "The race is between education and catastrophe," as if H. G. Wells had not said it first.

The number of physical exemptions for military service was huge because the men were so unfit. Householders in the country were shocked to discover that many of the Londoners foisted on them during the blitz were unaccustomed to bathrooms and indoor plumbing. The children had lice and skin diseases.

I WAS PRETTY WELL received in Britain because of my book on the emergence of modern American writing, *On Native Grounds* (1942). It was handsomely reviewed in the *Times Literary Supplement* by Denis Brogan, who invited me to visit him at Peterhouse in Cambridge University. Brogan was an aggressive, brilliant Irishman from Glasgow, the only assertively pro-American intellectual I met in this period; but he was pro-America by default, out of scorn for all the British academics and journalists he knew. Most of them he thought too "pink," and, besides, they were always putting America down because they knew nothing about it. Brogan never let me forget that after graduating from Oxford he had gone on to study at Harvard, and he knew things about America that even Americans didn't. Confederate Governor Wise of Virginia was related to Union General Meade, for instance, and once sent a young relative across the lines to Pennsylvania with a personal note. The best doctoral thesis in American history, moreover, had been written by Arthur M. Schlesinger Sr., on colonial merchants and the revolution.

Brogan at one time had a certain eclat as a historian of modern Britain—*The Rift in the Lute* was an early title—and France between Napoleon and Pétain; most of his books, though, were on American themes. He seemed to find his greatest intellectual pleasure in vilifying the left, and was among the few to support the magazine *Encounter* when its subsidy from the CIA was revealed. It astonished me that he was such a sorehead. Although he had Ernest Barker's old chair at Cambridge, he insisted that he should have been appointed to Oxford. "They" had not done right by him, no doubt because he was Irish Catholic in background. After one dinner at Peterhouse, he said to me of a Russian-born economist who had just left the room: "That man's a foreigner here and doesn't know it. I'm a foreigner here and I damn well do know it!" When a Frenchwoman at a dinner party said she was gratified by his splendid French, Brogan explained that he only spoke French well when he was drunk. Known for his memory and expertise in malice, he regaled me on the train from Cambridge to Liverpool Street Station by reciting morsel after morsel of personal and sexual gossip about Kingsley Martin, the fellow-traveling editor of *The New Statesman*. Brogan took conservatism to reactionary heights. Obviously let down by my person after reviewing my book so heartily, he suddenly blurted out with heartfelt irritation, "Now, you Jews . . ."

It seemed typical of me and my working-class background to find myself in Britain and not in the company of the irascible genius Evelyn Waugh, who was in Greece driving his superior officers crazy by insisting on claret at lunch ("I *always* have claret at lunch"). Waugh's *Handful of Dust* had properly terrified me into thinking it one of the great twentieth-century novels. I wanted to meet him, if only to see him as a spectacle on stage. I easily imagined the scene to myself: Waugh grumpily asking me the purpose of my visit and, when I hesitatingly entered into my well-rehearsed analysis of the Comic in *Decline and Fall* and the Grotesque in *A Handful of Dust*, his shudder as he rang for the butler and asked him to show this fellow out.

V. S. Pritchett, the English critic I most admired along with George Orwell, was also out of reach—in Germany for *The New Statesman*, writing about life there after the Allied crossing of the Rhine. Once to my indignation when I was at the *New Statesman* offices, I heard editor Kingsley Martin complain that Victor Pritchett's reporting from Germany, sensitive and beautifully written, was not political enough for him.

No, usually my companions were virtuously humdrum Labour blokes. I enjoyed the privileges of a second lieutenant in the gigantic dining hall reserved for American officers in a posh hotel. Then I would dutifully depart for the East End settlement houses to talk to the poor about Walt Whitman. In the wonderful ways of war propaganda, Whitman had become a representative American, just like Franklin D. Roosevelt.

G EORGE ORWELL was already important to me because of his "London Letter" in *Partisan Review,* the American journal that for decades exemplified the close connection between modernism and independent radicalism. Even the arch-conservative T. S. Eliot was glad to give PR his "Dry Salvages." John Dewey, Wallace Stevens, Tate, Auden, Gide, Silone, and many other great ones appeared in its pages, while the most intrepid of the New York intellectuals—Philip Rahv, Sidney Hook, Irving Howe, Clement Greenberg, Meyer Schapiro—made the magazine bristle with their attacks on Stalinism. But in London every time I went around to the *Tribune,* the socialist journal headed by the Labour

MP Aneurin Bevan where Orwell was literary editor, I discovered that Orwell was also off reporting from France or Germany or somewhere else trying to recover from the lung disease that in five years was to kill him. Once at the *Tribune* I came so close to Orwell's cubbyhole I could smell the rough shag tobacco that helped to undo him at the age of forty-six. But his cigarettes were as near as I ever got to George Orwell.

"Not one of us!" said a Labour Party secretary in Limehouse when, interviewing him on Labour's plans for postwar society, I asked him what he thought of Orwell. His name was apparently better known to Americans on the anti-Stalinist left than to most English and American readers before *Animal Farm* and *1984* made him world-famous. Orwell's column in *Partisan Review* described the impact of war on him with a kind of ferocious objectivity; the events he factually reported told their own story. Yet there was also a hot patriotic concern for the English people that impressed me all the more because at home, right next to Orwell in PR, the contentious Dwight Macdonald, a kind of moral anarchist who had a new political line every few years, was insisting that Hitler's was merely another imperialist war.

"Not one of us"? Orwell in *The Road to Wigan Pier* (1937) had written, "We are living in a world in which nobody is free, in which hardly anybody is secure, in which it is almost impossible to be honest and to remain alive . . . And this is merely a preliminary state, in a country still rich with the loot of a hundred years. Presently there may be coming God knows what horrors—horrors of which, in this sheltered island, we have not even a traditional knowledge." This prophecy was too severe for Labour. In *Homage to Catalonia* (1938) he described what I fondly thought of as our (his and mine) version of the Spanish civil war; there was homage indeed, to the Spanish anarchists and to the independent Marxist battalion, the POUM, in which Orwell had served along with other unaffiliated British radicals. Under Soviet pressure, in 1937 the Spanish government declared the POUM illegal. Wounded in the throat and in danger of arrest because he had supported the abandoned cause, Orwell fled Spain. I could feel his unyielding bitterness, quite unfashionable on the left in those days, about the Russian domination of the Loyalist cause. By its repression of the anarchist revolution in Catalonia and by its attempt to kill off all opposition on the left, Soviet Russia had given Franco his victory.

"Not one of us." To the solid union official representing the Labour Party in the slums of London, George Orwell—the author of such novels as *Burmese Days, A Clergyman's Daughter, Keep the Aspidistra Flying, Coming up for Air,* plus his personal experience of what really went on at the bottom of society in *Down and Out in Paris and London* and *Wigan Pier*—was just an intellectual and probably a class enemy as well. Never having read his books, the official knew only that Orwell was an old Etonian and, instead of going on to Oxford or Cambridge, had joined the Indian imperial police in Burma. Orwell was too independent a radical intellectual for the trade-union left and too downright honest for the fellow travelers. In 1944 his publisher Victor Gollancz was horrified by *Animal Farm*, Orwell's satire on the gross inequalities in the communist system. "I could not possibly publish . . . a general attack of this nature." For political reasons, many other publishers also rejected the manuscript, including Eliot at Faber.

In the dead of winter, before the Allies crossed the Rhine, I heard a great deal about the "reconstruction of society" in the army discussion groups, but there was an undercurrent of derision and despair to much of it. Whole units in the armed forces were planning to leave Britain for the colonies—*any* colony—in self-sufficient cooperative movements. The longed-for reconstruction of British society waited on the defeat of Hitler, and a Labour victory in the first postwar election seemed unthinkable in the face of Churchill's wartime domination. Even as winter yielded to the glorious spring of 1945, and the first

Michaelmas daisies sprouting in the bombed damp earth were featured on "Renascence" posters all over the city, much of the grime, violence, and deadly fatigue that were to go into *1984* became familiar to me under the rain of V-2s on London, the canned spaghetti and soup meat ladled out in the municipal kitchens for those who had been bombed out, the ferocious factory schedules that gave rise to the bitter saying, "Work and bed—might as well be dead."

In 1949 when Robert Giroux of Harcourt, Brace gave me a copy of *1984,* saying in a hushed voice, "This is the most important book we've ever published," I recognized that many details in the book describing the hardships of daily living came from 1944, not 1984. In the novel, thirty rocket bombs a week are falling on London but, as literary folk like to say, they are only symbolic. Yet the imminence of bombs was real enough. There is all the pain and fears of everyday life drawn from the war period—and there is Orwell's experience of Soviet repression in the Spanish civil war and his outrage at Stalin's choking of political and intellectual life behind the iron curtain. Even so, the book is more than a warning about a totalitarian nightmare in the future. It is the lament of a dying man about his dying society.

The right seized upon *1984* as a warning against communism. Leftists like C. P. Snow and the critic Raymond Williams hated the book because they saw it, in Snow's words, as a wish that the future would simply not take place. Both right and left were correct in what they saw as Orwell's political message, and both were wrong in charging that his message was nothing more than political. Orwell was an old-fashioned radical in the great line of English Protestant dissent. He raged against what William Blake, in a tradition that goes back to seventeenth-century religious sects, called "The Beast."

The Beast now was not the moral law or the established church, but the almighty state in its most coercive totalitarian form. And *1984* is certainly about the manipulation by the state of people's most commonplace habits of thinking. In *Homage to Catalonia* Orwell had described with rapture the anarchists' spontaneous "revolution from below" in Barcelona. For the first time, there was actually a society not just founded on principles but actually *living* equality, fraternity, and justice. Then that unique dazzling summer fell to the winter of state power in the name of Socialism, the most elusive of people's collective dreams. Political realism, state opportunism, and repression were becoming the political environment everywhere. Tyranny was the twentieth-century norm, all too imaginable by 1984 even in England. And the future was all too foreseeable in 1945 as Stalin took over eastern Europe.

What went wrong? Orwell noted almost casually,

in one of those polemical book reviews that make his collected pieces a treasure of literary journalism, the eclipse of the old sense of right and wrong that was founded on a belief in immortality, with its inherent notion of eternal justice. There was no cosmic authority to keep the human heart from hopeless despair. For as Orwell desolately said, with his usual honesty, it is not enough to have faith if you lack credulity. Desolation indeed, when individuals were in themselves so small, pitiful, and easily persuaded to lie; when in confronting their empty selves, people saw no reason not to lie for petty and glittery immediate advantage. Reality was anything you said it was. The act of lying was now the great political fact, which in *1984* led to the state's total rewriting of history. O'Brien the inquisitor forces Winston Smith to say (in terror of the rats he so feared) exactly the opposite of what he most cherishes. In the end Winston will submit with all his heart, will love Big Brother, not so much because he's frail but because he wouldn't know where to look for truth even if he remembered what it was. Long before *1984*, Hemingway in "The Snows of Kilimanjaro" has his dying writer lament not that he had lied so often in his life but that there was no truth left to believe in.

The pollution of language in ordinary discourse follows from the regimentation of language for state purposes in totalitarian societies, from commercial intimidation and advertising propaganda in morally regimented "democratic" societies. Orwell's most practical concern in *1984* was with the degradation of public language. Propelling it was the social wretchedness of an England that did rise to a degree of cooperation between the classes under the pressure of Hitler's war—the most moving political sight I have ever witnessed—but then stayed with the same poverty, the same primitive class-based obedience, the same resignation. In this sense Orwell remained a social rebel, but without hope. And in *1984* perhaps it is such fatalism, echoed in his reckless attempts to defy his certain death by fleeing to the worst possible wintry climates for a tubercular, that underpins his horror of mankind's servitude to power. It becomes power for the sake and enjoyment of power, as O'Brien says when he is torturing Winston Smith and at the same time dismissing all the reasons usually given to explain away the joy of dominating someone else.

Those who complained that the picture of totalitarian culture in *1984* was impossibly exaggerated were correct. The very idea of totalitarianism is an exaggeration, an annihilation of our natural sense of limits. Adolf Hitler is reported to have said in his "table talk," no doubt in a reflective moment over dinner, that the idea of personal happiness is gone.

Totalitarianism represented the triumph of a radical *idea* over nature itself, and the idea was what Nietzsche in his personally affirmative dream called the will to power. The triumph of the will, as Leni Riefenstahl called her shattering film of the 1934 Nazi rallies at Nuremberg, in all its programmed awesomeness replaced everything except the ruling party's images of its ultimate authority, thanks to the ecstatic acceptance of the crowd.

Orwell's *1984* is too narrow and manipulative to be in a class with other absolute visions of the human state such as *Gulliver's Travels* and *The Brothers Karamazov*. In its hysteria about a future rising out of the authoritarian controls that every society had to enforce during the second world war—Orwell died in despair over the fate of freedom, which in the end meant more to him than socialism—it sounds more like the work of a disabused intellectual than that of a novelist. And, we are aware, no one hates leftists more than an ex-leftist. We have only to think of those New York intellectuals who spent the first half of their lives as radicals in one party or sect, and the second half as neoconservatives with considerable influence on American political life and social thought.

Yet *1984* remains a great warning, like the brilliant tracts Orwell wrote in *Inside the Whale* or *The Lion and the Unicorn: Socialism and the English Genius*.

These are works distinguished by their lucid conversational style. The four volumes of his *Collected Essays, Journalism and Letters* are for me his most natural and satisfactory writing; everything there is so honest, sensible, rooted in his old-fashioned English sense of fact. Like the essays of Edmund Burke, Bernard Shaw, G. K. Chesterton, and Edmund Wilson, they resonate with the crises of the age that produced them. Like all great topical literary journalism, Orwell's essays have been absorbed back into their period, and thus remain a safer guide to the passion of that period than anything later historians have to say about it.

For Orwell the passion was all political. I was surprised when I read excerpts from the diary he kept in the first weeks of the war: he reported nothing but military campaigns. Not a word about himself or writing in England or the spirit of the people. You learn about the death of his wife Eileen on an operating table only from a letter to someone about other things. Early on, Pritchett said of Orwell that he had the tone of a wearied saint. Looking for some stray morsel of value in politics can weary the most obstinate conscience, and Orwell was all stalwart English conscience. But in 1945 Orwell was already weary to death. E. M. Forster said that Keats took his stand on "the small amount of good in the world," and that was the beauty of Keats. Orwell was too distracted by totalitarianism, torn asunder by it, finally to see anything else. His loss of credulity made an interesting contrast with the Scottish poet Edwin Muir, whose singular purity led to a spiritual revolution in my life (and not only because he translated Kafka).

I HAD GONE up to Edinburgh at Muir's invitation— he was in charge of British cultural services there—to talk to a small group about modern American poetry. Muir especially liked Robert Frost and Wallace Stevens. There was a poignancy to the man along with an aching good faith, a transparency about everything he liked and believed, which I can never forget. Muir had a seriousness of mind and a personal humility so unknown to Americans, especially the gaudy bureaucrats I had just left living it up in London, that he seemed to come from a world so far off it could have been in another galaxy.

In a sense he did. He was the son of poor farmfolk in the Orkney Islands northeast of Scotland; his wife Willa came from the Shetlands, which are closer to Scandinavia than to Britain. Muir's early life, which he described for me with the greatest simplicity and which he later put into an unearthly memoir, *The Story and the Fable,* was in a world that predated the industrial revolution, an inaccessible world, truly basic. The island waters still embraced "the drowned original of the soul." Orkney families had lived in the same place for hundreds of years. There was no real distinction between the ordinary and the fabulous: "The lives of living men turned into legend." He felt so close to the few objects he possessed that they were like magnets palpably drawing him close.

As Muir talked, I could hear someone in a room above us walking up and down in a fixed routine without stopping. Muir sadly explained that his son was full of anxiety after a brush with an automobile in the street, and it took the form of incessant pacing in his room. The family history was tragic. Muir's parents had been driven from farm to farm because of the exactions of a landlord he bitterly called in his poem of that title, "The Little General," always stalking about with a gun. The Muirs moved to Glasgow when he was fourteen. "The first few years after we came to Glasgow," Muir wrote, "were so stupidly wretched, such a meaningless waste of inherited virtue, that I cannot write of them even now without confused grief and anger." The family was so unused to industrial harshness and the terrible city slums that both parents and two brothers died there within two years of one another. Muir himself survived, despite illness and drab clerical jobs, by recalling, as if from dreams, the primitive, ageless world he had grown up with—all earth, water, and sky. His poetry

had the most intense power, unexpected in so gentle
a man. From "The Mythical Journey":

> First in the North.
> The black sea-tangle beaches,
> Brine-bitter stillness, tablet-strewn morass,
> Tall women against the sky with heads
>   covered,
> The witch's house below the black-toothed
>   mountain,
> Wave echo in the roofless chapel,
> The twice-dead castle on the swamp-green
>   mound,
> Darkness at noon-day, wheel of fire at
>   midnight,
> The level sun and the wild shooting shadows.

Muir's drive to educate himself gave him the cu-
riosity about foreign literatures that led him and
Willa to Prague and thus to Kafka. I had not yet read
The Trial when I met them. I did struggle unsuccess-
fully with *The Castle,* an allegorical labyrinth, but for
unconscious reasons that at least demonstrated some
literary intuition, I had been afraid to open *The Trial.*
Then as news began to seep into wartime England
about the mass killings, I realized that Kafka's fellow
Jews were actually living *Der Prozess*—first published in 1925, a year after Kafka's death.

When I left the Muir house to sight-see in Edin-

burgh and ended up at Holyrood Castle, once occupied by Mary Queen of Scots, I found myself in a
long, tormented conversation with a soldier in the
Polish exile army, who turned out to be a very bitter
Jew. Growing up in a Jewish enclave at the end of
the subway line in Brooklyn, I never dreamed that,
when I grew up and got to visit the castle of Mary
Queen of Scots, I would be led all over Edinburgh,
including its vilest slums, by a bitter Jew, verbally
lashed, forced hour after hour to hear the latest news
of the slaughter of Polish Jews and of Stalin's take-
over of Poland. My soldier said over and over, "I will
never get home!"

There was no escaping him and there was no
escaping *The Trial,* not in 1945. On April 15, a
British medical detachment stumbled on Belsen, hidden deep in the north German woods, to find typhus
raging among 40,000 starving, dying prisoners, and
13,000 corpses stacked on the ground. A London
Times correspondent was with them and sent back a
dispatch that began, "I have something to report that
lies beyond the imagination of mankind."

But that was a journalist on the scene. Back in
London, I read *The Trial* in the latest 1945 printing
on wartime paper (the Muirs' translation had first
come out in 1930). I could see that it was Kafka's
plainness, as I thought of it—a style so humble in
its simplicity that it seemed to be begging God for

permission to say even this much—which best served to point to all that was so unutterable, unanswerable, in the things being done to Joseph K. In Auschwitz, the Italian writer Primo Levi remembers asking a guard, "Why all this? Why?" Only to be told, "There is no *why* here."

That is the terror Kafka only imagined in *The Trial*. His friends laughed when he read his first stories to them; they were outside everything familiar (as yet) and were thus intentionally absurd—a perfect definition of humor, they thought, another *Alice in Wonderland*. Of course the strange illogic in Kafka's work frightened some people and made others furious. Edmund Wilson saw nothing in Kafka (as he saw nothing in Dickinson or Frost). When Kafka became all the rage, this was a serious mark against Wilson with the New York intellectuals. Harold Rosenberg maintained that Wilson couldn't be any good if he didn't like Kafka. Conversely, Bernard Berenson severely warned me in Rome in 1947: "There is a very small light of reason burning in the world. Mr. Kafka tries to put it out."

What Kafka caught was the unreasonableness of things made totally believable by what I call the humility of his language. The mind can describe many processes in nature, but sooner or later the mind, despite what science boasts, cannot be satisfactorily correlated with all that exists outside it.

This is the abyss that great literature fills, though never so fully that we cannot still hear the wailing of Job and Lear. A linear exactness in telling what happened to Joseph K. does not *explain,* as critics like to do. Kafka merely begins: "Someone must have been telling lies about Joseph K., for without having done anything wrong he was arrested one fine morning." He is left free to do what he can for himself. That is the most penetrating irony behind his every frustrated effort to persuade the law, the church, his neighbors, his would-be lovers, to find even an intercessor much less a lucid judgment on, or against, himself. So the book ends not only with his execution in the night, in darkness, without anyone to console or explain, but with the same senselessness:

> K. now perceived clearly that he was supposed to seize the knife himself, as it travelled from hand to hand above him, and plunge it into his own breast. But he did not do so, he merely turned his head, which was still free to move, and gazed around him. He could not completely rise to the occasion, he could not relieve the officials of all their tasks; the responsibility for this last failure of his lay with him who had not left him the remnant of strength necessary for the deed.

And who was that unproviding figure? Probably the same voice out of the whirlwind that, when Job was most wretched, told the sufferer how insignificant he was compared to Himself, the almighty all-providing Creator.

There is no *why* to be asked of this God either. That is the "unanswerable," Kafka's theme. With the sublime cruelty of genius, he had the nerve to write it as a parable for those who one day might read him. Remember, however, that he ordered his friend Max Brod to burn his manuscripts.

I N EUROPE because of my book on modern American prose, I wanted fiercely to learn Europe. It turned out that Europe was crazy to learn the latest American writers. So I went to Paris, on my first airplane ride, just before Bastille Day in 1945 to address the first postwar congress of French professors of English and American literature. The grand boulevards were lined with stalls; emaciated whores teetered in wooden platform shoes stalking every GI; food was still so scarce that my host English teachers had nothing to give me for lunch but some grassy vegetables. My honorarium was a school text of Pascal. But the same week, when *On Native Grounds* came out in France, the publisher threw a fantastic lunch, steak and champagne, waiters in white gloves. Sergeant Albert J. Guerard (later Professor Guerard of Harvard), sitting next to me, was amused: "The food is black market, and you know who's paying for all this? The American embassy!"

The French intellectuals I met didn't know whether they loved America more than they hated it or hated it more than they loved it, but either way they were obsessed with us. There would soon appear tough and gory pseudo-American novels written by French pulp novelists, with titles like *Je crache sur vos tombeaux* (I Spit on Your Graves). Coca-Cola was so abhorred as a symbol of degenerate American capitalism that one student climbed to the top of Notre-Dame to drink off some Coke as the most dramatic show of blasphemy. But at the hotel in the Rue d'Astorg taken over by the American military, thirty-two-year-old Albert Camus announced to his more literary GI admirers, "I love Faulkner because I too am a Southerner. I love the dust and the heat."

The copy of *L'Etranger* I bought that day in Paris has long been in tatters, but I have only to pick it up to feel again, beyond the first shock of a style so cold and detached, the embrace of a cosmic philosophy, a wholly new point of view. In the very title, Stranger, Outsider, I sensed a determination to remake us in thought, to see man in depth, in the scale of the whole universe, and no recent American book ever did that to me. The hero is not just outside conventional morality, but makes a point of it. Meursault demonstrates in his flat idiom and every physical gesture that he believes in not-believing. This little novel, published at the height of the war in 1942, was evidently the record of a conversion away from the old humanism. It did not simply portray a way of life, as with the Hemingway who had so obviously inspired Camus' artificially bleak style; it was a way of seeing. Of course Hemingway wrote from a stance of American stoicism, finding titles like *In Our Time, A Farewell to Arms, Death in the Afternoon,* and *A Way You'll Never Be* to show, as on a movie screen, the world of war that had broken the hero's heart.

But that was mere romantic disillusionment next to the total reasoning that made Camus' stranger, the outsider to our ways, remain so obstinately detached even before the guillotine. In America only writers grounded in a crumbling but still respected religious culture (Melville, Whitman, Dickinson) agonized like Camus and other Europeans over the need for a world-historical view that would express the diminishment if not the loss of God. At the end of *The Trial,* in the depths of Joseph K.'s agony at having to be his own executioner and to die all alone, inexplicably and meaninglessly, there is an unheard cry: "Where was the Judge whom he had never seen? Where was the High Court, to which he had never penetrated?" Reading that I thought of *Moby-Dick:* "Where is the foundling's Father hidden?" And when I turned to the school text of Pascal the professors of English had given me for my talk on all those American writers the French had missed during the war, I realized that the advantage was mine. Nothing I could tell them about the brilliance of this one or the style of that one could compare, for me, with the words in Pascal's *Pensées* (25.16–17). Translating from the French:

> When I consider the short duration of my life, swallowed up in the eternity before and after, the little space that I fill and can even see, plunged into the infinite immensity of spaces which I do not know and which do not know me, I am frightened and astonished at being here rather than there; for there is no reason why here rather than there, or why now rather than then. Who put me here? By whose order and direction are this place and time destined for me? . . .
>
> The eternal silence of these infinite spaces frightens me! (*Le silence éternal de ces espaces infinis m'effraye!*)

Camus' text, though stridently atheist, has this in common with Pascal: it is a protest against the socialized obligation to close our eyes to the abyss where we really live, where we conceal our dread and rarely recognize how little we know. And in the spring of 1945, with the victory over Nazism somehow diminished by the sense of human defeat and shame at the mountain of corpses left by the war, I understood Camus' protagonist to incarnate more than Europe's universal moral fatigue. Meursault's whole life is a protest against the standard language of concealment. In 1955 Camus wrote a preface to an edition of *The Stranger* for American students. I was not surprised to hear him say of his character, a murderer, that he is condemned mostly because he doesn't play the game, refuses to lie:

> Contrary to appearances, he does not want to simplify life . . . A profound passion, though a tacit one, moves him—a passion for the absolute and for the truth. The truth at stake is as yet only negative, the truth of being and feeling. But without this truth, no conquest over oneself and over the world will ever be possible . . . *The Stranger* is the story of a man who, without any heroic posturizing, is willing to die for the truth . . . I tried to symbolize in my character the only Christ of which we are worthy.

Only a European could have so commemorated a novel written in the midst of Hitler's war. The European difference, as I saw it then, was in the kind of philosophical thinking that went the limit, was not afraid of absolutes, was grounded in a traditional culture that had gone through endless attacks since the Enlightenment on religious faith and continued to lament the inability to believe.

There were more encouraging voices. I kept by my side in England a passage from Alfred North Whitehead's *Science and the Modern World,* a book from which Wilson in *Axel's Castle* had taken his argument in tracing the origins of modern literature to romanticism. Whitehead's extraordinary passage about the meaning to him of religion marked an epoch in my life. Wilson the bristling agnostic—he was always telling me, "We must live without religion"—would have cared less.

> Every great religious teacher has revolted against the presentation of religion as a mere sanction of rules of conduct. St. Paul denounced the Law, and Puritan divines spoke of the filthy rags of righteousness. The insistence upon rules of conduct marks the ebb of religious fervour. Above and beyond all things, the religious life is not a research after comfort. I must now state, in all diffidence, what I conceive to be the essential character of the religious spirit.
>
> Religion is the vision of something which stands beyond, behind, and within, the passing flux of immediate things; something which is real, and yet waiting to be realised; something which is a remote possibility, and yet the greatest of present facts; something which gives meaning to all that

passes, and yet eludes apprehension; something whose possession is the final good, and yet is beyond all reach; something which is the ultimate ideal, and the hopeless quest.

. . . Gradually, slowly, steadily the vision recurs in history under nobler form and with clearer expression. It is the one element in human experience which persistently shows an upward trend. It fades, and then recurs. But when it renews its force, it recurs with an added richness and purity of content. The fact of the religious vision, and its history of persistent expansion, is our one ground for optimism. Apart from it, human life is a flash of occasional enjoyments lighting up a mass of pain and misery, a bagatelle of transient experience.

Coming from one of the world's leading mathematical logicians—coauthor with Bertrand Russell of *Principia Mathematica* (and Russell thought all religion a mere illusion)—this pleased me because it was so personal, tentative, and distinctly un-American. Back home the true believers boasted that Americans were attending church, synagogue, and mosque in record numbers, but that was more of a social phenomenon and there was a punitive emphasis on sexual misconduct. The American writer, as D. H. Lawrence observed, tends to be harsh, stoic, and isolate. The radiance in Emerson, Thoreau, and

Whitman, still glimmering in Dickinson but without the full assurance of "a world elsewhere," had been a last effort to keep something alive in a society that was losing its sense of history as an on-going spiritual effort, that was indifferent to anything standing in the way of its newer faith in progress. The last great American writer to mourn the demise of religion was William James. He made it severe and clear in *The Varieties of Religious Experience* that no matter how many God-intoxicated saints had come through nervous crises to the Supreme Being, "God" was no longer an option for William James, whose own nervous crises had threatened his sense of identity.

The churches in America were tribal, and religious anxiety expressed itself in the need to belong with one's own. Eliot, "the king" for many of us, had gone to England to find even a trace of the respect for authority he could not find in his family's liberal Unitarianism. But Eliot's stilted pronouncements as a pillar of the established church could not conceal the fissures in his personal makeup that turn his poetry into a haunting, ever more pressing search for his lost connections with childhood, America, a past. When I had a chance to interview him in his office at Faber and Faber about my own work on popular education—in his early days he had actually lectured for the Workers' Education Association—he was hungry for news of America, of Harvard friends we had in common. President Roosevelt had just died, and when Eliot asked "What's this Truman like?" I couldn't resist saying, "You ought to know, you both come from Missouri."

American writers at the opening of this century ached for the lost world of belief, as in Wallace Stevens' poem "Sunday Morning." What followed—and a good thing as it turned out—was a recognition that the development of the United States was the best possible subject for a novelist. Yet it had to be the poets here who recognized, as Joyce and Proust across the sea did in the novel, that the immediate data of consciousness were great new literary material. But the poets, in the absence of tradition necessary to poetry, could only react against their society's belief in its unique invincible progress and felt left behind by America's intoxication with itself.

The twenty years between the world wars, the most creative of times for American artists, anticipated in our literature and art what Europe experienced after 1939. The most critically intense in its death throes was the idea of God, of any leftover idea of God. Of course the "death of God," as Nietzsche had almost satirically first proclaimed it, adding that news of it would take a long time to reach most men, had long been everyone's preamble to modern thinking. It was a special favorite in America with writers who had been not a little scathed by orthodoxy in childhood—Mark Twain, Theodore Dreiser, Stephen Crane, Wallace Stevens. As Stevens puts it in "No Possum, No Sop, No Taters": "He is not here, the old sun / As absent as if we were asleep . . . It is here, in this bad, that we reach / The last purity of the knowledge of good." He phrases it more languidly, or should I say conceptually, as in exquisite line after line in "Sunday Morning" he portrays death as the mother of beauty, the death of our oldest beliefs merging into the lonely truth that we now have nothing but nature, day and night, an "island solitude, unsponsored, free."

It was not religion, as in America, but the absence of God, a fixed point, that threatened Europeans to their very core. Tolstoy lamented, "One cannot live so! One cannot live so!" To the French writer Simone Weil (1909–1943), there was such an obvious, urgent connection between the death of Europe in the second world war and the eclipse of a God embodying the absolute good that her death was virtually self-inflicted (she refused nourishment and medical treatment). It is not too much to say that she died of a failure to live the absolute.

Like many American intellectuals still more or less on the left, I first encountered Simone Weil when I read her now famous essay, "The *Iliad*, Poem of Might," in Dwight Macdonald's invaluable magazine *Politics*.

No one would have guessed from the title that the author was another ex-radical, that she went to Spain to help the Loyalist cause during the civil war, and that in the midst of the war, in 1938, she did not hesitate to express in a letter to the Catholic novelist Georges Bernanos (who on Majorca had witnessed the mercilessness of the Franco forces) her horror at the gratuitous killings by the Loyalists:

> The point is the attitude toward murder. Never once have I seen, either among the Spaniards themselves or among the French who went there to fight or to amuse themselves (the latter often being gloomy, harmless intellectuals), anyone who expressed, even in private conversation, repugnance or disgust or even disapproval of unnecessary bloodshed . . . Men who seemed courageous, when dining with friends, would relate with warm, comradely chuckles how many priests they had killed or how many "fascists," a most elastic term . . . When men know that they can kill without fear of punishment or blame, they kill; or at least they smile encouragingly at those who kill.

The essay on the *Iliad* was begun in 1939 and published in Marseilles after the French surrender to the Nazis. By then Weil, with a degree in philosophy, had lost her teaching job because she was a Jew. She wrote a letter to the Vichy minister of education, asking for her job back, but got no reply. (Part of the discomfort so many feel about Weil stems from her peculiar renunciation of Judaism; in her letter to Vichy she said, "the Hebraic tradition is alien to me.") Now she was waiting with her parents for passage to America.

There was nothing about her personal situation in the essay, though its theme is that in war, and perhaps not only in war, the human condition is so condensed by violence that the aggressor is finally crushed along with his victim. It begins: "The true hero, the real subject, the core of the *Iliad,* is might *(la force).* That might which is wielded by men rules over them, and before it man's flesh cringes. The human soul never ceases to be modified by its encounter with might, is swept on, blinded by that which it believes itself able to handle, bowed beneath the power of that which it suffers." Before the concentration camps were disclosed to the outside world, she understood that force makes a thing of its victims. "There where someone stood a moment ago, stands no one. This is the spectacle which the *Iliad* never tires of presenting." Hector becomes a thing dragged in the dust behind a chariot. A Trojan warrior, naked and helpless, facing a sword aimed directly at him, for a moment still deliberates, strives, hopes.

Motionless Achilles considered. The other drew
near, seized
By desire to touch his knees. He wished in his
heart
To escape evil death, and black destiny . . .
With one arm he encircled those knees to
implore him,
With the other he kept hold of his bright lance.

But the man already knows he is dead. When Priam
enters as suppliant, he too encircles Achilles' knees
and kisses those hands, "terrible slayers of men,
which had cost him so many sons." This was the
king of Troy. "The spectacle of a man reduced to
such a degree of misery freezes almost as does the
sight of a corpse." Even Achilles shivers at the sight,
for a moment.

But no prisoner of the Nazis would have thought
it useful to beg for life. Achilles will not be stopped
from killing, but at least he "considers" and knows
that he and his foes share the same killing fate. The
sword he thrusts into the Trojan rules him as much
as he rules his victim. Of course we have come far
from the code of heroic honor to which Achilles and
his foes are pledged. The classicists who under-
standably faulted Weil's *Iliad* as Virgilian in attitude
rather than Homeric, too admonitory and pessimis-

tic, false to Homer's joyful demonstration of the warrior cult, missed the real subject of the piece: Hitler's war. It needed a moral extremist like Simone Weil to anticipate in 1939–40 all the inexpressible horrors yet to come.

Even my easy use of the word "extremist" cannot convey the fanatical, pitiless, totally isolating and self-destructive idealism of this woman. Briefly a refugee with her family in New York, she was tormented because so many people were starving in France. She bullied her friends among the Free French to get her to London. There, sick with tuberculosis and starving herself in emulation of her compatriots, she absurdly demanded to be parachuted into France so that she and other would-be nurses could care for the wounded in the field, whatever the cost to their lives; she thought a death right then and there entirely fitting. De Gaulle himself called this crazy. The Free French in London thought her impossible and put her off by asking her to write a memorandum on what could be done after the war to regenerate France. This became the disregarded but remarkable document, *L'Enracinement* (The Need for Roots).

Frustrated in her every effort to get to France and do something tangible for her people, Simone Weil, thirty-four years old, died in England in 1943. The quick French surrender in 1940 had left the country with ineradicable guilt and humiliation, as did the trucking of Frenchmen to Germany as slave labor for the Nazis. The Vichy regime openly favored a German victory. So many of the French collaborated with the Nazis, informing on Jews and partisans and profiting from the occupation, that in the bad conscience after the war and the sour bravado of atheist intellectuals, Simone Weil's life and thought were claimed for the church by French Catholics, who knew about her fascination with Christianity. She had steadily affirmed her need for intellectual independence as her main reason for staying out of the church: "Of course I knew quite well that my conception of life was Christian. That is why it never occurred to me that I could enter the Christian community." I suspect slightly that she was intellectually too proud to become just another convert, indistinguishable from millions of the faithful. The church on its part was troubled by her rejection of Judaism, which led her to trace Christianity back to Greek philosophy rather than to its biblical Jewish past.

Selma Weil, Simone's mother, admitted when I visited her in 1950 that she thought her daughter excessive, for all her gifts, and would have preferred the poor child to be "just happy." Here I have to explain why, although I confess myself relieved never to have met Simone Weil in person, her writing startled and moved me at a time when the war had left me with a painful distrust of people in power, of the official world, of the overbearing, relentlessly radical intellectuals glibly rationalizing and in a sense excusing the Holocaust and Stalin's reprisals against repatriated Russian prisoners of war. The world was so insane now that only a conscience that had left the rest of us behind, like the terrified Pip in *Moby-Dick* jumping from the boat into the open sea, seemed equal to a fresh act of love for man and the world besotted by man. Melville wrote in the chapter called "The Castaway," as Pip goes mad after drifting alone in the vast ocean: "The intense concentration of self in the middle of such a heartless immensity, my God! who can tell it?"

Weil was truly such a castaway when she died apart from her parents, her beloved France, even the Free French she had finally given up on. But in her resurrected notebooks and personal testaments—*Waiting for God, Gravity and Grace, The Need for Roots, Letter to a Believer, Supernatural Knowledge,* and many others (she would write all day, never moving from her chair under the most appalling refugee conditions)—I saw a charity absolutely unknown in my immediate world, an intelligence that owed nothing to authority and worldly prudence, a personal sense of God's reality and truth so natural to her that it could shock you into taking it seriously as well.

In exile she counseled her countrymen "first of all to choose everything that is purely and genuinely good, without the slightest consideration for expediency." She said of nationalism that the state had become "a cold concern which cannot inspire love, but itself kills, suppresses everything that might be loved; so one is forced to love it, because there is nothing else." By 1940, even such forced patriotic love was gone from her pro-German countrymen. The effect of this on the French soul was of great concern to Weil. As a radical in the thirties, she did manual labor at the Renault auto factory and was immersed in the smallest details of working-class life. She noted that "the sense of justice is . . . strong among workingmen, because they are always under the impression that they are being deprived of it." Though she spoke of herself as a Christian, she would sharply add: "Christianity is, apart from a few isolated centers of inspiration, something socially in accord with the interests of those who exploit the people." Nothing in our time is more familiar than modern man's sense of rootlessness, but like Wordsworth a century before, only Simone Weil could ascribe it to a lost contact with the world's recollection of divinity.

This loss she blamed on the Judeo-Christian conception of God as a person. As people came to doubt the reality of a single divine figurehead, they lost their faith altogether and believed the world to be nothing but determinism—she called it "necessity"—a different order of being from their old hopes and desires and one that science alone had the conceit to interpret. Her abhorrence of a world construed simply as necessity was central to her compulsion for personal intervention against the public abuses of power by social bodies. What finally kept her outside the church, she explained in *Waiting for God (L'Attente de Dieu)*, is that "so many things are outside it, so many things that I love and do not want to give up, so many things that God loves, otherwise they would not exist." This led to distress over the Catholic rite of excommunication; always defending sufferers, she would have to remain beside those proscribed by the church. Similarly, though a Jew forced to flee for her life from Hitler, she would protest with characteristic indignation against the belief that God could have "chosen" the Jews or any people for any purpose whatever; she was equally outraged at the Romans' contempt for their slaves, which she believed had carried over into the modern brutalities inflicted on workers, heretics, prisoners, and the colored races. This is what drove her to factory work and to Spain during the civil war where, again characteristically, she (like Orwell) testified to the cruelties perpetrated by "her side."

What struck me most in her crowded gallery of

judgments, harsh and sublime, was her saying in *Waiting for God:* "Those who are unhappy have no need for anything in this world but people capable of giving them their attention . . . The love of our neighbor in all its fullness simply means being able to say to him, 'What are you going through?'" Attention she called the "contrary" of contempt. This included "a recognition that the sufferer exists, not only as a unit in a collection, or a specimen from the social category labelled 'unfortunate,' but as a man, exactly like us, who was one day stamped with a special mark by affliction. For this reason it is enough, but it is indispensable, to know how to look at him in a certain way."

We cannot go toward God, she said, we can only wait, with an attentiveness that has no particular object to gain. That is the highest form of prayer: *L'attention sans objet est la prière sous sa forme suprême.* From the moment I came across this, I knew I had been given a wonderful gift. "Attentiveness without object" said more about the foundations of poetry than anything else in my knowledge. I could imagine Emily Dickinson, when she ventured into her Amherst garden, being attentive in just that way, beginning a poem without knowing *what* she was beginning.

But can we live that way with the unresponsive machine that the world has become? To everything and anything waiting for us, we would attend, caught up in the stillness we experience only in exhaustion, as after making love. Then we might resume the closeness to the world that we dimly trace only in memory. And then such truth as is given us to know we would not only write in books. We might just live it.

WALKING the London streets in the exhilaration of that perfect May, when the war finally came to an end and couples were openly making love in Hyde Park, I remembered that William Blake had said these things, that I was walking streets he had walked:

> The fields from Islington to Marybone,
> To Primrose Hill and Saint John's Wood,
> Were builded over with pillars of gold,
> And there Jerusalem's pillars stood.

In the socialist bookshop in Charing Cross—I was there to pick up the great Sloss-Wallis edition of Blake's prophetic books, for a new assignment to edit the Viking Portable Blake—a placard on the wall quoted Bernard Shaw: "Only in books has mankind known perfect truth, love and beauty." The placard hung uneasily from a nail, dislodged but a survivor of the bombing nearby. Shaw was still alive in 1945, even if his Victorian uplift was not. The totalitarian age had passed him by, and his arrogant need to shock had led him to praise Stalin and to make excuses for Hitler because he, Bernard Shaw, the eternal man of letters, still thought humanity in desperate need of his instruction.

Nothing was now so old-fashioned about Shaw as his fixation on creative evolution—the progress of man from the slime to the socialist superman. His positive dislike of sex made too many of his plays conversation pieces. To see his *Caesar and Cleopatra* after Shakespeare's *Anthony and Cleopatra* is a joke. Shaw thought that the only passion left in man was social protest. The passion of his one great woman character, Saint Joan, is for God. But Shaw's prefaces were better than his plays because there he could confess the lonely religious nature of his radicalism. His favorite "novel" was *Pilgrim's Progress*, Joan his only sweetheart. Everywhere in his manifestoes, this extraordinary autodidact propounded the belief of which his socialism was the smallest part: there are profound *purposes* to existence still undisclosed.

Blake would have thought Shaw's dream of revolution only so much wistful prose. What I saw around me in London as the war ended was truly the marriage of heaven and hell. Blake's imagination as "vision"—religious, sexual, political, above all poetic and artistic—gave me new life as I worked on

Blake in Blake's own city. A stranger there, often dismally lonely among the English people (but not among their poets), I was haunted by lines from Blake's poem "London":

> I wander thro' each charter'd street,
> Near where the charter'd Thames does flow.
> And mark in every face I meet
> Marks of weakness, marks of woe.
>
> In every cry of every Man,
> In every Infant's cry of fear,
> In every voice, in every ban,
> The mind-forg'd manacles I hear.

When I got back to New York, I walked through my own city and wrote a book about it.

chapter 3

After
the War

The century might have been a good one had man not been watched from time immemorial by the cruel enemy who had sworn to destroy him, that hairless, evil, flesh-eating beast—man himself. One and one make one—there's our mystery. The beast was hiding, and suddenly we surprised his look deep in the eyes of our neighbors . . . I saw the beast still living—myself. One and one make one—what a misunderstanding! Where does it come from, this rancid, dead taste in my mouth? . . . It is the taste of the century. Happy centuries, you who do not know our hatreds, how could you understand the atrocious power of our fatal loves?

—Jean-Paul Sartre, *The Condemned of Altona* (1960)

I N THE 1930s I often met left-wing painters in Greenwich Village, down on their luck like everyone else, who for a pittance from some federal arts project were painting murals in post offices and other public places, celebrating the American dream in a style not uninfluenced by what the Soviets called socialist realism. But now, breathing in new personal friskiness from the boom that came in with the war, and profiting by their contact with the avant-garde European painters who came over as refugees, they became radical in the most imaginative sense, and threw off the shackles of commonplace realism in favor of abstract expressionism. To the astonishment of everyone but the artists themselves, New York replaced Paris as the world's art capital.

I liked to be around painters. They were not so much given to grandiose solitude as the writers I knew, were lustier and more convivial. When you visited Saul Bellow in his tiny room on Riverside

Drive, you had to stand on the toilet to get a glimpse of the Hudson. Delmore Schwartz lived in a squalid box on Greenwich Street, an address that should not be confused with Greenwich Avenue. There, when not writing, Delmore spent his time cursing his friends, especially Bellow. Bellow had raised a fund to get Schwartz some urgently needed psychiatric care, and when Delmore refused the care and claimed the money for himself, Bellow restored it to the donors. That earned him the poet's eternal enmity.

Delmore's room on Greenwich Street was surely the room that Raskolnikov had holed up in to dream of murdering the old pawnbroker. Poverty alone could not account for such a room; it was not so much uncomfortable or dirty or damp, dark, and constricted; it was the kind of room that could have been chosen only by someone with assured knowledge of all the murderously bad rooms put aside and carefully preserved by the heartless State for poets to die in. It needed a character long practiced in disaster to discover a room like that.

And there he was, buried alive up to his piercing eyes in "betrayal," not so much talking as spilling over in his reedy voice a headlong rush of words, which seemed to engage every muscle behind the surface of his face as he contorted in the rage of his unhappiness. His face was still marvelous at the end, in his awful sickness; he talked with his face. Like his poetry, it had a habit of transcending him. Here is the first measure of his Bear (the beast within) poem from 1938:

> The heavy bear who goes with me,
> A manifold honey to smear his face,
> Clumsy and lumbering here and there,
> The central ton of every place,
> The hungry beating brutish one
> In love with candy, anger, and sleep,
> Crazy factotum, dishevelling all,
> Climbs the building, kicks the football,
> Boxes his brother in the hate-ridden city.

The last time I saw Delmore was on a Saturday morning in 1962, four years before he died. He was insatiably bitter, arguing against people with the same passionate logic (he had been trained in philosophy) with which he used to argue for or against certain books. But the face was still remarkable. When relaxed for a moment, it was just as noble as it had seemed to me thirty years before, when I first saw him in a train going up to Boston. Then I was struck by the immense intellectual devotion in it, the fine distraction, the sensitivity coming through the frantic gestures.

Delmore was the most gifted person in the *Partisan Review* household. He was "our poet." He wore his talent on his sleeve, along with his passion for Joyce and Eliot, his love of philosophy as well as his addiction to poetry, the excited discoveries he was making in those years of teaching at Harvard. Even in his twenties he had authority. Although he talked so fast that he swallowed his words, he would grow marvelously serene between gulps of argument and friendly smiles, with the unmistakable look of a man possessing his own legend. He stood for something, and he knew it.

"A poet shouldn't be that unhappy," W. H. Auden laughed as he looked at Delmore's photograph on the cover of his last book, *Summer Knowledge* (1959). By that time the poet was more than unhappy—he was in hell. He was drowning in a depression special to himself, hopelessly caught up in a tangled web of trying to *prove* that injustice, betrayal, was everywhere being directed to him. He had once joked, "Just because a man is paranoic doesn't mean his enemies aren't real." The worse things got, the more wildly would he argue and argue. He was a prisoner of his own superb intellectual training, a victim of the logic he respected so much. He was of the generation that does not come easily to concepts of the absurd, to the contented nihilism that can enjoy the best of all times in the worst of all possible worlds.

Poor Delmore, even when impaled on his *idée fixe,*

lacked the saving grace of madness that some poets need in order to enter their vision. He was never lost enough in that rich private dream, that seeming unreality, which can become to the eye of genius the only "real world," as Blake described the imagination. For all Delmore's irrationalities, his work is tight, controlled, intellectual, always respectful of classical good sense and order. Lost he was, but not "lost" in the demonic poetic tradition. His anxiety was that of the ex-radical idealist who still reveres the rationality of the world. He was not a seer or a visionary of the "lost traveller's dream under the hill," had none of the holy madness that Yeats claimed for Ireland itself. He was a New York Jew who liked to say, "Europe is still the biggest thing in North America"—meaning its literature and art and the Russian revolution—an ex-radical so unbalanced when his beloved *Partisan Review* switched to a conservative pro-American ideology, away from its old skeptical modernism, that once I even heard him rail against the quiet antifascist Ignazio Silone (who had made some criticism of American foreign policy).

O N MY OWN after returning from England, no longer married, I was even more helpless during the severe housing shortage I encountered. But I trusted some painter to rescue me. Painters have a genius for discovering the large real estate their work demands. They would always surface in remote unfashionable neighborhoods that many writers I knew sniffed at, since they had grown up there. Finally a friend of Bellow's, Arthur Lidov, a painter who had prospered in commercial art, let me have his old home and studio on Pineapple Street in Brooklyn Heights. Eventually he took a studio adjacent to that of Mark Rothko, and it was my old landlord, as Bellow called him, who was one of the first to discover the dead man when Rothko most horribly hacked himself to death in 1970.

My encounters with Rothko in the days of his fame were few but unforgettable. He owned an old carriage house in the East 90s, and one night he had a big, noisy, frolicsome party there, from which he removed himself, like Jay Gatsby mooning over his inner life. He stood on the steps outside, talking to me with the most guarded, frozen expression on his face while saying the most remarkable things. His reminiscences were all of his loneliness in America, not that he thought better of his first ten years lived in tsarist Russia. In the thirties, a student of mathematics at Yale, he would have to hitch-hike his way back home to Oregon. The roads were so empty during the depression that one afternoon, praying for someone, anyone, to come along, Rothko saw a pitiful old jalopy lumbering up the highway. Unbelievably it stopped. The scrawnily bearded old man behind the wheel looked out at Rothko and growled, "I seen you a long way off and I says to myself, 'That's a Jew! He may beat me up but he won't rob me.' Get in!" Another time, returning from Europe on one of the last transatlantic liners, Rothko couldn't stand his loneliness, went up to the bar, and said to a perfect stranger, "Let's talk!"

When Rothko was not just depressed but "in great sorrow," as he put it, when something impossibly terrible brought him down, he said he turned to Shakespeare's tragedies. That really knocked me out. In the early 1950s, I had to my surprise become a full-fledged professor at distinguished universities here and abroad, after my first teaching experiences at City College's summer and evening sessions, Black Mountain College, and the New School for Social Research. Not one of my colleagues in any English department ever admitted turning to Shakespeare, as Macbeth kept turning to the witches, for some kind of reassurance in this uncertain world. Shakespeare was never a personal matter, only professional, someone to be competitive about. Shakespeare was a highly technical area, like the inside of your car.

I never knew why Rothko, grown rich and world-famous, was so unhappy, or why he talked as a matter of course from the bottom of his soul while standing, a desperate millionaire, apart from the noisy party in his own house. But the mystery of his unhappiness was like the mystery within and around those large rectangles, swimming in interior spaces, increasingly dimmed (as Rothko neared his end) by muted colors and black borders. "I have to paint large so as to keep it intimate," Rothko said. Intimate with what? Not with the painting itself, in its unmistakable homage to the silence of the universe. Not for Rothko the savage piling up of matter from anywhere that *The New Yorker's* art critic Harold Rosenberg called action painting, and that he proudly described as "fucking up the canvas." That was New York all right, when Rosenberg could present Jackson Pollock comparing himself to Nature, which then took you back to Whitman's "I am large, I contain multitudes." No less ambitious but a little more selective, Rothko told a painter I knew that he wanted a picture to "glow like a Rembrandt."

Rothko's longing for intimacy haunted me, as did his round, spectacled face knotted in pain behind all those plain-spoken admissions about the loneliness he felt in the world. He was looking for something beyond the merely personal (which in our time means psychological), and I, without knowing anything much about him, dared to call "some reason for our existence in this world." Some reason not just for his own existence, nerve-driven as that was for him, but perhaps for the existence of the world itself.

Rothko, in all his anguish, remained something of a political protester at heart. When offered a stupendous fee to paint murals for the super-posh Four Seasons restaurant in midtown Manhattan, he was so revolted by one meal there, the expense-account crowd and the prices, that he split up his work and sent it elsewhere. But like other radicals of the thirties, in the delirious postwar atmosphere he was searching not for a replacement of the God that failed but for a way of looking at the world in its entirety. Rothko called it whatever he called it not only because he was clumsy with words, but because he was a painter trying to condense the universe into visual images. Evelyn Waugh said about becoming a Catholic, "I believe in it all. What I can't understand is why God made the world in the first place."

The first problem in my metaphysics course at college had now become my own: "Why is there Something rather than Nothing?" Alone in my painter's studio on Brooklyn Heights, unable for weeks to take down the savagely imagined portraits of concentration-camp prisoners behind barbed wire that my landlord had painted and left on the wall, I was unsettled in every sense. The opening lines of Dante's *Inferno* spoke to my condition: "In the middle of our life, I found myself in a dark wood, for the straight way was lost." In the winter of my discontent, freezing in Pineapple Street, obsessed by the war against the Jews and Stalin's grabbing what Hitler had left, I found myself identifying with that terrible voice in Dostoevsky's *Notes from Under-ground:*

> I am a sick man. I am a spiteful man . . . being overly conscious is a disease, a genuine, full-fledged disease. Ordinary human consciousness would be more than sufficient for everyday human needs—that is, even half or a quarter of the amount of consciousness that's available to a cultured man in our unfortunate nineteenth century, especially to one who has the particular misfortune of living in St. Petersburg, the most abstract and premeditated city in the whole world. (Cities can be either premeditated or unpremeditated.)

It was my particular misfortune to be caught in New York—but Brooklyn Bridge was two blocks away. I came alive walking it every day and trying in my journals to do justice to the old city still huddled on either side. What made my coming home meaningful at last was my nearness to that bridge and my joy every time I went back to Hart Crane's poem about it, the greatest New York poem after Whitman's "Crossing Brooklyn Ferry." *The Bridge* (1929) is a modern epic, as perfectly expressive of a twentieth-century poet's need to make a myth for the future out of the iron and grit of daily living as Whitman's need, in the century before, to transcend the ruins of the old religion in a myth of joining Brooklyn and Manhattan, island and island, earth and water. His new myth would make for recognition of him by those of us yet unborn:

> Closer yet I approach you,
> What thought you have of me now, I had as
>   much of you—I laid in my stores in advance,
> I considered long and seriously of you before
>   you were born.

Crane would have liked to be that personal, that loving, in print, but he didn't know how to escape the isolation of his homosexuality; Whitman glorified his in the name of togetherness—my city, my people, my America. New York for Crane was no longer the neighborhood it had been for Whitman. Even Columbia Heights facing the harbor, where he slunk home after furtive adventures, was no neighborhood for him. He seemed to have had little confidence in his power to receive love. But how he loved John Roebling's bridge as the great Other, and what sinewy strength he gave to celebrating it! He starts the poem in a rhetorical mode, like someone practicing a foreign language, but his words pierce

through that hard-won, tortured ornateness to catch
us in an overwhelming tide of feeling:

> O harp and altar, of the fury fused,
> (How could mere toil align thy choiring strings!)
> Terrific threshold of the prophet's pledge,
> Prayer of pariah, and the lover's cry—
>
> . . . . .
>
> Under thy shadow by the piers I waited;
> Only in darkness is thy shadow clear.
> The City's fiery parcels all undone,
> Already snow submerges an iron year . . .
>
> O sleepless as the river under thee,
> Vaulting the sea, the prairies' dreaming sod,
> Unto us lowliest sometime sweep, descend
> And of the curveship lend a myth to God.

What can we call feeling like that? It is all entreaty,
with none of Whitman's pride. It is all prayer from
someone in dire need. I liked to read aloud Crane's
opening eleven stanzas ("Proem: To Brooklyn
Bridge"), which often left me slightly exalted, something rare enough in my experience of current
American poetry. But I never experienced the full
power of the emotion packed up in Crane until I
heard Allen Ginsberg read the same stanzas to my
students at Stony Brook, some twenty-five years ago.
He made the words resound through the classroom,

waking up young souls who had never been roused by a poem before. In the swoops and falls of his steady, deep voice, with the unashamed volume and practiced declamation I have heard only from Russian poets reading aloud, Ginsberg communicated a bond with Crane that was defiant—more assertive than the words on the page had seemed, but revealing a voice within every word that was new to me. You couldn't miss the strong personal identification. Crane's experience of life had led to suicide (he too jumped into the open sea), but in Ginsberg's reading Crane was reclaimed, championed, "vaulted."

To my delight, I was assigned by *Harper's Bazaar* to do a piece on Brooklyn Bridge with the great French photographer Henri Cartier-Bresson. In 1946 the bridge was still anchored in the iron age. Walking in from Manhattan I saw nearby fire escapes decorated with sculptured figures of prize fighters out of the old *Police Gazette*.

The genius of Cartier-Bresson's eye transformed me, and I saw New York as color, line, and form. He was excited by the wooden boardwalk down the center of the bridge, a unique promenade from which you could see harbor and city at once. "It breathes!" Cartier-Bresson said in praise of the boardwalk. "See how it breathes!" We got on so well that we thought about doing *le tout* New York in a book. But it never worked out, and I began writing one of my own, *A Walker in the City.*

It was ambitious, a sort of personal epic journey all around New York, starting with morning in Pineapple Street, the blaze of midtown at noon and in rush hour, the crowds, the museums, the markets and libraries. The third section was about Sunday in New York, full of color, poignancy, and what I thought was dazzling prose. The middle section, "The Old Neighborhood," consisted of some dozen pages of childhood memories, jotted down in a flood of recollection in one afternoon. It didn't seem grand enough as a subject by comparison with midtown and New York on Sunday: I was a critic with a critic's weakness for ideas. Once I had noted in my journal, after a particularly sad Friday evening meal with my parents, who had never moved: "Every time I go back it all feels like a foreign country." But I finally came to my senses, and in *A Walker in the City* I began: "Every time I go back to Brownsville it is as if I had never been away." My natal country was not behind me at all. When E. B. White removed to Maine from Manhattan, he described himself as "homesick for loneliness." That was my case now, my particular good fortune. The past had broken out in my heart, as Rilke said of poetry, and I was thinking in color, luxuriating in physical sensations that something in me remembered. My explosion into so much personal history had at least this excuse: it came from someone taken up in history, someone who was in history—like all his people—even before he was born.

On Pineapple Street I was bombarded by the dialogue and loud background music emanating from the little movie house across the street, where on hot nights the projectionist kept his door open. In the midst of this and the shouts from drunken fights outside the waterfront bars, I found myself doing the revisions needed of her English in Hannah Arendt's *Origins of Totalitarianism.* The Boston publisher who had an option on the book asked a Harvard professor of government for his opinion. The professor was irritated by the book, perhaps because it so flatly linked Nazism with Stalinism, and he advised them to turn it down. Hannah was bewildered. Fortunately I was then a literary adviser to Harcourt, Brace, which owed its great list to the boldness of Alfred Harcourt. In 1919 Harcourt heard from his first literary adviser, Walter Lippmann, that Felix Frankfurter at the Versailles conference was much impressed with the economist John Maynard Keynes, who was writing his prophetic criticism of the Versailles treaty, *The Economic Consequences of the Peace.* Harcourt cabled Keynes his acceptance of the book unread. Whereupon the grateful Keynes brought over to Harcourt his friends Lytton Strachey, Virginia Woolf, and others of the Bloomsbury crowd.

So I brought *The Origins of Totalitarianism* to Robert Giroux, the firm's wonderfully sensitive chief editor, who stayed up all one night to finish his reading. "A great book," he said. "Of course we'll publish it." Hannah was on her way.

When I met her in 1946, she and her Protestant husband Heinrich Bluecher were so poor that they rented out a room in their apartment on Morning-side Drive, a street that faced a park it was suicide to enter. Like Randall Jarrell and Robert Lowell, who were also to find Arendt an irresistible teacher and an intellectual force, I was charged up by the example of her intense German cultivation. Jarrell, too young among southern poets and critics to be still mourning the Confederacy, was the ultimate culture-vulture. To me his poetry, based on literary ideas, was not up to his criticism, which was murderously sharp. Conrad Aiken complained publicly about the cruelty of Jarrell's reviews. But Randall at his truest was really an enthusiast, and he had the nerve to come out for Walt Whitman—imagine a southerner defying the New Criticism like that! He said he would pay to teach, and it didn't matter where. He was so responsive to what Hannah Arendt could teach *him* that I couldn't tell if he was in love with her or with German. He ended up tackling *Faust*.

With typical bravado he explained, "I'm too busy translating *Faust* to learn German."

"Cal" Lowell's genius was in his antennae. He could sniff out, in a poem whose language he could barely read, the nervous graphic force he had first demonstrated in *Lord Weary's Castle* and was now to capture in *Imitations,* triumphing over his own ignorance and mistakes in the literal versions given him by friends. Like Jarrell, he basked in Arendt's admiration. Other poets needed praise; Lowell expected adoration. Having been praised in his early period by Pound and Santayana, and finding himself irresistible not just to the many confessional women poets in the Boston area but to Flannery O'Connor at Yaddo, there was no holding him back. He caused great hurt during the McCarthy era by accusing the executive director at Yaddo of taking in left-wing writers and having sinister contact with the Soviet embassy. He was so proud of his name that when he claimed conscientious objection during the war, even though his terrible eyesight would have kept him out, he had the nerve to wire President Roosevelt that Lowells had always fought for their country but for moral reasons he, Robert Traill Spence Lowell Jr., could just now not offer his services. So he went to jail.

I always forgave Lowell for taking on superior airs. His talent in a generation of poet wimps was vivid and strong, even if the learned allusions with which he began his career were derived from the southern- ers he adored so much. I was frequently entertained by his grand gestures. Only Lowell was capable of saying of Jewish writers who were just as saturated in American life and literature as himself: "They have finally unloaded their European baggage." His poetry during his Catholic period was powerful, for all its ornamental refinement. But with *Life Studies* his poetry got to me for its depth of feeling and the wit, irony, and literary cunning with which he man- aged to convey his bereft inner life. I never thought that frantic disciples in the confessional mode, such as Anne Sexton and my Smith student Sylvia Plath, captured—even wanted to capture—Lowell's im- mensely sophisticated ease in knowing when to rein in, his upper-class training in controlled conversa- tion. As in "Skunk Hour":

> The season's ill—
> we've lost our summer millionaire,
> who seemed to leap from an L. L. Bean
> catalogue. His nine-knot yawl
> was auctioned off to lobstermen.
> A red fox stain covers Blue Hill.

The most surprising thing to me about Lowell's writing was his occasional reproducing of a courtly literary tradition quite unremembered by American writers. The formidably elegant prose memories of "91 Revere Street" in *Life Studies* could have been written by Walter Savage Landor in 1838. Yet his best poems were direct in the appeal he made from his up-and-down manic depression. He became ill at the same time every year. In "Waking in the Blue," a poem about his residence at McLean's (Harvard's psychiatric hospital), he wonderfully, casually ends, "We are all old-timers, / each of us holds a locked razor." He was graphic in a way that gave him a real audience for the poetry, not just a gallery of connoisseurs.

One night, after a very liquid dinner at my home, he suddenly remembered that he had a talk to give that very night at the New School for Social Research. We foolishly took a Broadway bus to get us to 12th Street from the West 80s. Some Columbia students on the bus recognized Lowell and gathered around to express admiration and ask questions. He was in heaven. This was in the middle of what I called his Thomas Hardy period. Talk of *imitations*. He expounded to the students his full faith and expertise in poetry exactly as the thundering old countryman Hardy might have done it. The performance was great, and so enticing that we never got that night to the New School.

I too was enthralled by Hannah Arendt's presence and was indebted to her, as I was to exiles like Paolo

Milano from Rome and Erich Heller from Prague, for advancing my education. *The Origins of Totalitarianism,* unlike so many interpretations of the Nazi regime, saw it as a deliberate and possibly irreversible break with tradition. Everything had been turned over so completely and savagely that, unless you understood the full nature of this revolt against all preceding humanisms, you couldn't know why it had to express itself in a totalist ideology and manifest itself through terror. In her culminating chapters on the parallel police systems in Germany and the Soviet Union, she argued that there was no essential difference between Hitlerism and Communism, whatever the contrary declarations of their beginnings.

The book was better received by literary people than by specialists in the many subjects it covered. It had the force of revelation, announcing a new dark period in history. Arendt's expressiveness in a second language was extraordinary. Her "sense of an ending" was so strong that the harshly brilliant structure she built up in her last chapters on the parallel between Hitler's and Stalin's systems, their arbitrary use of condemnation and terror, the central importance of the secret police, could be read as a stupendous literary image, like Dante's Inferno. But in her writing about Russia, there was not a single reference to the historical actualities of tsarist society. She believed she was writing a new philosophy of politics, a field into which she had been intellectually compelled by her exile, but she was marked by her rigorous training in the classics and philosophy. She took her doctorate at Heidelberg under Karl Jaspers, writing on Augustine's conception of love. She liked to repeat Augustine's saying, "Love means that I want you to *be*." In the first edition of her book, the painful sense of totalitarianism as "the burden of our time" led her to end with Saint Paul's words to his fellow prisoners at Acre: "Do yourself no harm, for we are all here."

But we were not all here. The campaign against the Jews had forced her to leave Germany right after Hitler took over in January 1933. Her book begins with the roots of nineteenth-century racial antisemitism, which replaced the old Christian promise of safety through conversion and meant in effect that all Jews had to die. When I met her in 1946, she was directing an organization concerned with returning to devastated Jewish communities the religious and cultural treasures stolen by the Germans. As a refugee in Paris, she had worked for a group trying to get children into Palestine. But her profound emotional concern with the fate of Jews was not matched by respect for Judaism or the synagogue. There was always conflict in her between the Jew and the German: she lamented the friends and associates she had lost; at the same time, nothing about being in a new country and using a new language could diminish her intellectual pride and self-assurance. She did not need to say that she was one with all those amazingly creative German Jews, from Heine, Marx, Freud, and Kafka up to her friends Walter Benjamin and Hermann Broch. She was not a Christian, but her primary allegiance was to the great tradition of European philosophy. Even Nietzsche had described Christianity as Platonism for the masses. Hannah's inner world was grounded in this tradition, modified by the syntheses that were always being replaced but never quite abandoned by rebels like Marx and Nietzsche. I didn't know it then, but Heidegger, who had been her lover when she was his student, remained an obsession through all her years in America. And Heidegger was nothing without his thought. No matter how questionable his character and his politics, he was Heidegger. After all, nobody on the Upper West Side of New York was capable of saying that the business of philosophy is to listen to the silence of existence.

With profound German thinking as her background—and she never let you forget its ties to Greece (even Dr. Karl Marx had identified the advancing proletariat with Prometheus)—and carrying on the lofty mission of German philosophy, Hannah Arendt explained that Nazism was not just an atrocity but a terrible uprooting, a mocking challenge to all our timid faith in "civilization." Hitler did not hesitate to boast of the New Order and the end of personal pursuits. The existence of such an undoing had to be explained over and over to modern liberals, who ascribed Nazism to some breakdown in economics or to the nature of German society. Arendt's tightly knotted sentences thus operated as refutation after refutation of the conventional wisdom. In the *Origins* she was the traditionalist as gadfly, and then she would go on to make a sophisticated point that only a philosopher could make. She spoke with the authority of the past, not as an original thinker but as a critic battling shallow modern misconceptions of the central human problem. The bond between the great tradition and the individual was sundered, and it was up to a new philosophy of politics to repair it. Otherwise, as she put it in her most penetrating pages, the lasting effect of the overorganized bureaucratic state would leave the individual not in solitude, which was creative and impossible under total domination, but in loneliness.

My debt to Hannah Arendt beyond anything else was that she had named the radical evil behind Nazism. But the Heidegger she could not escape—least of all in her second book in English, *The Human Condition* (1958), with its familiar Heideggerian thesis that the Greeks made a cult of contemplation, never an ethic of labor—was not my dish. The haughty, unworldly side of Heidegger's thinking had not kept him from joining the Nazi Party and throwing his old Jewish teacher Edmund Husserl out of the University of Freiburg, or from hating the modern world for its "technology," or from identifying wisdom with the primordial thinking of the pre-Socratics. After the war he told his former student Herbert Marcuse that Germany's forced cession of east German lands to Poland could be likened to the Holocaust.

For me the most attractive German philosopher was Nietzsche, and Jean-Paul Sartre was the philosopher-artist who most resembled Nietzsche in his expression of unlimited freedom and the almost contemptuous command of his style. New York after the war became Sartre's second-best audience. His very titles were a challenge: *L'Etre et le Néant, La Nausée, Les Chemins de la liberté, Huis-clos, La Putain respectueuse, Les Main sales*. He was brilliant in his impudence, vehemently opposed to "seriousness" even as he sounded the depths of a metaphysical solitude as drastic as Pascal's but prouder, never anguished. For Sartre, ours was the century of creative denial, and he betrayed not the slightest longing for salvation. He seemed to throw over all the constraints by

which we conventionally live and replaced them
with the vigorous gestures and free choices of a man
totally alive and participant in the world.

Nausea, published in 1938, had a healing, astrin-
gent effect on me after the war. Sartre was a writer
who peremptorily challenged you to change your
life—and for a season I succumbed. Naive as it may
seem now after Sartre's apologies for totalitarianism
and the red terror, that book in an age of alienation
remains altogether affirmative in its picture of Existence, pure being, the ecstasy of just being alive. It
resonates like Wordsworth at his most inspired in
"The Prelude." Just as the greatest romantic poets
recovered from the disruption of the old religious
synthesis by seeing in Nature the essence of being,
so Sartre's protagonist Roquentin, confronting the
"treeness" of a tree, is released from the agony of
trying to make total sense of the world, to hold it all
together by force of intellect.

Roquentin is a historian weary of his profession.
He is struggling with a book about the eighteenth-
century Marquis de Rollebon, a character as hard to
get hold of as himself. Except for a scratchy record
of the song "Some One of These Days, You're Gonna
Miss Me, Honey," which he obsessively listens to in
the cafe where the patronne distractedly allows him
to make love to her while discussing cafe business,
Roquentin has nothing but his research to hold him

to life. His personal diary is an effort to capture consciousness at any cost: "I must always be ready, otherwise it will slip through my fingers. I must . . . carefully note and detail all that happens . . . Anyhow, it was certain that I was afraid or had some other feeling of that sort. If I had only known what I was afraid of, I would have made a great step forward."

Roquentin's excruciatingly concentrated effort to keep intact is his sickness, his nausea. So much is always happening around him, how can he keep it all from flowing past? How can he get a handle on anything as a guide to everything? Of the slippery Marquis de Rollebon, he says: "I am beginning to believe that nothing can ever be proved. These are honest hypotheses which take the facts into account; but I sense so definitely that they come from me, and that they are simply a way of unifying my own knowledge. Not a glimmer comes from Rollebon's side."

Then, discontentedly sitting in the park, bemused by the roots just under his bench of a rotting chestnut tree, frightened by the beastliness of this black, knotty mass, he has a vision:

It left me breathless. Never, until these last few days, had I understood the meaning of "existence" . . . I was thinking of *belonging* . . . Even when I

looked at things, I was miles from dreaming that
they existed: they looked like scenery to me. . . .
And then, all of a sudden, there it was, clear as
day: existence had suddenly unveiled itself. It had
lost the harmless look of an abstract category: it
was the very paste of things, this root was kneaded
into existence. Or rather the root, the park gates,
the bench, the sparse grass, all that had vanished:
the diversity of things, their individuality, was
only an appearance, a veneer. The veneer had
melted, leaving soft, monstrous masses, all in dis-
order—naked, in a frightful, obscene nakedness.

The philosopher unchained? The unprecedented
wonder of pure Existence, Being, Inherence, *Dasein,*
coming into our lives? *Nausea* remains a wonderful
novel of ideas—and is indeed more than that. In
1950 it was one of the twelve novels selected by a
special jury in France to receive the Grand Prix for
the best fiction of the first half of the century. Along
with Proust's *Swann's Way* and Colette's *Vagabond,*
Sartre's novel remains resonantly itself, and even for
its author (Sartre was only thirty-three when it appeared) complete in itself.

But the more Sartre took possession of French
letters in the postwar murk, pouring out treatise
after treatise, fiction after fiction, play after play, and
in each instance serving as theorist for those who
reveled in theory, the more he refuted the ecstasy of

pure being proclaimed in *Nausea.* Only poetry and music of the most profound *Innerlichkeit* can come close to the merest hint that the temporality in which we have our being, which is *our* being, can be expressed.

Sartre's idea of freedom was writing—thinking at the highest pitch. He felt himself free to be as unsponsored, unconventional, libertine, and revolutionary as he liked. The past did not exist for a man who was always celebrating life *now* as the clay from which to model a perfect collective future. Except when Russian repression in Hungary or Czechoslovakia regularly surprised him, Sartre believed in communism. His sense of "perilous freedom" for the individual somehow did not extend to the prisoners massed in the gulags. He wrote a wonderful autobiography, *Les Mots,* directed against his bourgeois, idealistic grandfather. In his hatred for the French bourgeoisie in general, Sartre defied the government ban on the incendiary Maoist paper, *L'Ami du peuple.* The most famous writer in France made a point of distributing copies on the streets of Paris. When urged to have him arrested, President de Gaulle said, "We tried that with Villon and it didn't work."

It seems odd that Sartre and Heidegger and Céline, like so many supremely gifted European writers, were partial to totalitarianism. They had such a deep sense of the wrongness possessing Europe that they thought to counter it by supporting "strongmen" like Pétain (Céline), Hitler (Heidegger), or Mao (Sartre). The tyranny did not matter. Europe *thought* in revolution, up or down, left or right, and sometimes all of that at once.

O NLY TWO American writers I knew had a sense of the radical evil that had burst upon the century—Saul Bellow from Chicago and Flannery O'Connor from Milledgeville, Georgia, ten years his junior. They were both so rooted in their contrary religious backgrounds, and each had such an unswerving, deeply engraved view of the world, that it amused me to think of one trying to do justice to the other.

The self-assured Bellow did not like to admit that there were other writers. When Hannah Arendt joined his Committee on Social Thought at the University of Chicago, and of course lectured him as she did the rest of us, he was outraged by such presumption and dismissed her in *Herzog* as "canned Weimar sauerkraut." The reclusive, deeply ailing O'Connor—she died at thirty-nine of lupus—recoiled from any view different from what was for her the central incarnate truth of the Host. Fellow southerners like Truman Capote and Tennessee Williams made her sick; literary folk from the ghastly northeast she caricatured as "interleckchuals," in her novel *Wise Blood*. She was so inflexible in her standards that her own parish priest, driving me up to see her after I had spoken at a nearby college in Georgia, remained in the car during my brief, tight visit, saying that her disapproval of his usual light reading matter made him afraid to see her out of church.

The narrowness in both Bellow and O'Connor was to their advantage as artists in America. The raging prosperity of the postwar period, the all-enveloping cheapness of popular culture (with paperbacks mass-manufactured like toothpaste and toilet paper), the GI bill and the unprecedented state and national support of education, had left no misgivings among liberals about the utter shallowness of American life. Harold Rosenberg's "herd of independent minds," the conformists in the huge new universities, soon found ideologies necessary to their vanity. The worst episode in human affairs, as Churchill described the Holocaust, went unremarked in English departments. The New Criticism, with its exclusive airs in dissecting the language of poems especially suited to its complacent agenda, demonstrated, not for the last time in the innocent history of poetry in America, the truth of Thomas Mann's saying that only prose writers get exiled.

Bellow would have none of this suburban smugness. In his second novel *The Victim*, significantly dedicated to an exiled intellectual (Paolo

Milano), Bellow imagines a very ordinary man, Asa Leventhal, numbed by the temporary absence of his wife and the heat of a New York summer, who is suddenly accused by a man he barely remembers, Allbee, of getting him fired and ruining him just because he's not a Jew. The most wonderful part of the book is that the bewildered Leventhal, without admitting to Allbee's charges, becomes mesmerized by the man's grievance. He recognizes a pointed determination in life superior to his own, and thus accepts the guilt thrust upon him without understanding it; he becomes the real victim. He allows the homeless Allbee the use of his apartment, and throws him out only when he mocks Leventhal's own loneliness by using it for sex. In the end—unlike the self-execution of Joseph K. in *The Trial,* which does not remove the guilt he never understands and is not meant to understand—normal life reasserts itself after the summer crisis three years before. It is a brilliantly satiric conclusion. Outside a theater Leventhal encounters a rejuvenated Allbee, who is no longer interested in him. Allbee is at peace: "I'm not the type that runs things. I never could be. I realized that long ago. I'm the type that comes to terms with whoever runs things. What do I care?" He rushes off without answering Leventhal's final bewilderment: "Wait a minute, what's your idea of who runs things?"

It bothers me that *The Victim* is not better known.

Bellow himself has belittled it as only a second novel, part of his apprenticeship. Asa Leventhal may be the last of his protagonists who is not the voice of Bellow's own intensely speculative intelligence. Most of the novels after *The Victim* turn around his deep readings of himself. Norman Mailer is richly talented in another way: he is the born novelist of society, so fascinated by its corruption and violence that he seems propelled to imitate its every appetite and to ride its roller coaster. But Bellow grows ever more impervious to the mechanics of American society and its screaming injustices. He has always given me the impression of a man trying to fathom himself under a providence that owes its effect on him to its very unfathomability. He is for me the only serious novelist of Jewish extraction, as it is politely called, who has this sense of God as *his* fate. In one of his best novels, *Mr. Sammler's Planet,* the old man, who escaped from Nazis shooting Jews huddled in a mass grave by crawling through the bodies piled on top of him, prays to God about his dead nephew: "He was aware that he must meet, and he did meet— through all the confusion and degrading clowning of this life through which we are speeding—he did meet the terms of his contract. The terms which, in his inmost heart, each man knows. As I know mine. As all know. For that is the truth of it—that we all know, God, that we know, that we know, we know, we know."

Bellow's bond with the intransigent Catholic O'Connor lies in this sense of obligation to the unseen, taking it up to a point when the unseen becomes real. Mary McCarthy, a lapsed Catholic, once told Flannery that she thought of the Host as a symbol, "and implied that it was a pretty good one." O'Connor describes the incident in a letter of December 16, 1955, to a friend, continuing: "I then said, in a very shaky voice, 'Well, if it's a symbol, to hell with it.' That was all the defense I was capable of, but I realize now that this is all I will ever be able to say about it outside of a story, except that it is the center of existence for me; all the rest of life is expendable." We can hear Simone Weil in this.

But is there another American writer who, even professing the same thought, would say this with the same disdain for others and—in speaking for herself—the same willingness to die for what she believes? Of course O'Connor was living with death much of her short life. But there is a severity, a compactness, to her faith exactly like the tone she takes to her characters. Everything is all of a piece with her, which is the last thing I would say about most of the people I know (especially the writers).

When in 1971 Farrar, Straus and Giroux brought out *The Complete Stories of Flannery O'Connor,* that word "complete," I thought, summed up author, book, life, and her approach to art. The driving characteristic of her mind, and therefore of her style, was to find people complete in the smallest gesture, or in the involuntary action of a microsecond, which decided a life forever. She could put everything about a character into a single look and make a story out of that character alone. She described people with the same finality with which she flatly claimed to know the distance from earth to heaven and hell. People for her were complete in their radical weakness, incomplete by being necessarily human.

So drastic a view is correspondingly dramatic, if you can prove it in your writing. There are rare lapses into editorial moralizing, as near the end of one of her best stories, "The Artificial Nigger," but for the most part her relentlessness holds. Her genius is in the sharp focus of her concentration. People are made absolutes, knives without handles. Hazel Motes all too believably blinds himself in *Wise Blood*. Old Mr. Fortune, in "A View of the Woods," loves his granddaughter so deeply and identifies her with himself so wildly that she amazes him one time by balking his wishes; trying to whip her, he kills her. The young son of the dissolute city couple in "The River" is taken by his babysitter to participate in a country baptism and later drowns trying to find his new friend Jesus in the river. From story to story we read: "He seemed mute and patient, like an old sheep waiting to be let out." Or "The rest of his face stuck out like a bare cliff to fall from." Or "When he finished he was like something washed ashore on her, and she had made obscene comments about him, which he remembered gradually during the day." There is a deadliness of observation without cruelty, comic because the various details are so telling about people who are notable only in their conformity: "Mrs. Watts' grin was as curved and sharp as the blade of a sickle. It was plain that she was so well-adjusted that she didn't have to think any more."

Incredibly, Flannery O'Connor would have been almost seventy by now. Of course her work has long seemed uncontemporary in its refusal of everything but the intrinsic human situation. We live in such an age of fragmented loyalties and self-loving commentary, with everybody doing their own thing, that her sense of the absolute can seem meaningless just now. Yet, perversely, I've always thought of her as our one classic in late twentieth-century American fiction, meaning that she transcended the circumstances in the South that made her possible but is still the best guide to those circumstances.

There she was: an extremist Irish Catholic locked up in the Bible Belt. In viciously anti-Catholic Klan country, she was celebrated posthumously as a true daughter of the South. And she was herself so locked up in her afflicted body that we can understand why experience as well as faith made her dwell on the

Host: "This is my body, this is my blood." She touched the bone of truth that is sunk in our own flesh. Sometimes she could lose herself in a story that rested its weight squarely on dramatic action. But fiction by her rules depended on an unyielding sense of our limits, and the limits could be raised only by death.

In "Greenleaf," the great story of a woman killed by the bull that her resentful, inefficient farmhand, Greenleaf, is always letting out, the woman finds herself staring at the "violent black streak bounding toward her as if she had no sense of distance, as if she could not decide at once what his intention was, and the bull had buried his head in her lap, like a wild tormented lover, before her expression changed . . . and she had the look of a person whose sight has been suddenly restored but who finds the light unbearable."

A UDEN WROTE in his "Homage to W. B. Yeats" that "poetry makes nothing happen," but such was certainly not the effect that Czeslaw Milosz had on me. And while Robert Frost was right to say that poetry is what is lost in translation, no modern poet I read in translation gives me so strong a sense of *recollection* as Milosz does; the original shines through. John Bayley, the excellent Oxford critic who reads Polish, says of Milosz: "A poet so good that he can be translated is a supreme paradox, one which many poets today, and readers of poetry, would refuse to recognize, so strong is the tendency now for poetry only to congeal and inhere in the carefully exploited accuracies and idiosyncrasies of a language" (*New York Review of Books,* June 4, 1981). Of course it helps that what you read in English is without ornament—plain, direct, always quiet. When I read Milosz I can actually hear his voice: whimsical, sorrowfully emancipated, never excessive in language or tone even with the terrible things he has to write about, and yet full of infinite regret, *lacrimae rerum,* the everlasting tears of things.

From his teaching post at Berkeley in 1969, he wrote this poem, "Calling to Order":

> You could scream
> Because mankind is mad.
> But you, of all people, should not.
>
> Out of what thin sand
> And mud and slime
> Out of what dogged splinters
> Did you fashion your castle against
>   the test of the sea,
> And now it is touched by a wave.

What chaos
Received bounds, from here to there.
What abyss
Was seen and passed over in silence.
What fear
Of what you are.

It shows itself
But that is not it.
It is named
Yet remains nameless.
It is coming to be
But has not begun.

Your castle will topple
Into the wine-colored
Funereal sea,
She will assuage your pride.
Yet you knew how
To use next to nothing.
It is not a matter of wisdom
Or virtue.

So how can you condemn
The unreason of others.

(Collected Poems, 1988, pp. 244–245)

But in Warsaw, 1943, in the midst of the horror
(the city the Nazis occupied in 1939 they destroyed
in retaliation for the 1944 uprising), Milosz thinks
of the Campo dei Fiori in Rome, once a field of

flowers, then a square where the heretic Giordano Bruno was burned, thinks of "baskets of olives and lemons, / cobbles spattered with wine / and the wreckage of flowers." But here, in wartime Warsaw, the music from a nearby carousel drowns "the salvos from the ghetto wall, / and couples were flying / high in the cloudless sky." Milosz does not say, does not have to say, that when people leaped from the ghetto windows to escape deportation, some Poles on the other side of the wall cheered them on: "Jump! Jump!" I think no other contemporary poet has written more affectingly about what went on right in front of him, so to speak, than Milosz did in "A Poor Christian Looks at the Ghetto." This is a poem he translated himself, and instead of predictable sentiment we hear:

Bees build around the honeycomb of lungs,
Ants build around white bone.
Torn is paper, rubber, linen, leather, flax,
Fiber, fabrics, cellulose, snakeskin, wire.
The roof and the wall collapse in flame and
   heat seizes the foundations.
Now there is only the earth, sandy, trodden down,
With one leafless tree.
(Collected Poems, p. 64)

Enion laments in William Blake's *Four Zoas:* "What is the price of Experience? do men buy it for a song? / Or wisdom for a dance in the street? / No,

it is bought with the price / Of all that a man hath:
his house, his wife, his children." Milosz has written
a moving book about his debt to Blake, *The Land of
Ulro* (1984). Ulro in Blake's system is the inhuman,
material world—space, error, science, the void, the
world of death—from which the spiritual imagination leads us to poetry, with its revelation of another
order of being. Ulro is certainly where this Polish
poet lived, and in a sense still lives observing the bay
and bridges from his house high on Grizzly Peak
Boulevard in Berkeley. We all live in the land of Ulro.
It is the endless struggle of our consciousness to rise
above it—Milosz would say *through* it, overlooking
nothing that chains us to all those temptations in
our culture that would deny a higher form of being—that is the source of poetry.

Milosz overlooks nothing of where he is now and
where he has been. This man who survived the Nazi
occupation of his country, then served its communist
regime as a diplomat just long enough to write *The
Captive Mind,* that classic report on the inflictions of
communism, stood up at Harvard University in 1982
to give the Charles Eliot Norton lectures. "Poetry"
suddenly took on a Slavic vehemence and political
importunity quite unfamiliar to American poets and
critics of poetry, and would have alarmed the genteel
Professor Norton, friend of John Ruskin and Henry
James.

Milosz said: "All my life I have been in the power

of a daimonion [demon], and how the poems dictated by him came into being I do not quite understand. That is the reason why, in my years of teaching Slavic literatures, I have limited myself to the history of literature, trying to avoid poetics." So much for all those pedagogue-critics who, themselves incapable of writing poetry, glibly explain as they take their equally innocent students over a poem word by word "what makes poetry work."

The sense of his own background overwhelms Milosz. Remember that this was written before the collapse of communism:

> My corner of Europe, owing to the extraordinary and lethal events that have been occurring there, comparable only to violent earthquakes, affords a peculiar perspective. As a result, all of us who come from those parts appraise poetry slightly differently than do the majority of my audience, for we tend to view it as a witness and participant in one of mankind's major transformations. I have titled this book *The Witness of Poetry* not because we witness it, but because it witnesses us.

What follows often reads like a report from hell, "not hell's first circle, but a much deeper one." Milosz sees a West-East axis in poetry drawn from contrasting human experiences. If he thinks our writers more fortunate, he also, like his hero Dostoevsky, thinks them pitiable. He draws fervently on the terrifying experiences of Polish poets in our time. Far from apologizing for poetry that may often be thought too extreme in the West, he just as fervently believes that the elemental strength of poetry, its ancient ritual quality, is realized when an entire community is stricken: the supposed schism between the poet and the larger human family disappeared in Poland under the Nazi occupation. "Poetry became as essential as bread."

There is obviously a great divide in Milosz's mind between what he calls our "alienated" poetry, full of introspective anxiety and artifice, and the kind of poetry written under Nazi and Communist tyranny, where "a peculiar fusion of the individual and the historical took place, which means that events burdening a whole community are perceived by a poet as touching him in a most personal manner. Then poetry is no longer alienated." Here Milosz misunderstands our alienation, even if he does not misjudge it. In his journals for 1987, published as *A Year of the Hunter,* he contrasts Simone Weil's belief that time is the greatest mystery to the American absence of metaphysical thinking, our obsession with sex and violence, the financing of our movies by corporate crocodiles. "To what extent can one think completely nakedly; that is, rejecting all imagination higher than physiology? One should ask prostitutes about this."

American poets, our writers generally, are anything but indifferent to the cruelties, injustices, and unstoppable violence of our society. None of us could ask in the 1990s what Robert Frost blithely asked in the 1920s: "How can you write the Russian novel in America so long as life goes on so unterribly?" The "Russian novel," if that still means anything, is being lived all over this country in poverty, racial conflict, homelessness, drug addiction, and the increasing numbers of so-called redundant workers thrown into the streets every week by one technological replacement after another. Nowhere are writers so sensitive to abuses of sex, race, and class. Nowhere are writers so inflamed by issues. But if they are alienated, and many profess to be, they are alienated not from society but from social thinking, of the kind that is content to curse dead white males and rejoice in the loss of tradition.

In a 1981 interview Milosz said he was most influenced by Simone Weil because of her deep concern with evil:

> I have a very clear, very strong feeling of opposed forces of good and evil . . . Western civilization is losing that distinction: Everything can be explained; everything is relative . . . I do not see a great chasm today between believers and nonbelievers because all these things are in a very strange state. We are going through a profound change of mentality and imagination. We are all afflicted . . . I am searching for an answer as to

what will result from an internal erosion of religious beliefs.

That says it all. Except on specific social, political, and psychological issues, where we are mighty crusaders, we no longer know what to think. "The most religious nation on earth," according to statistics on church attendance, is devoted to public gestures in a declamatory political farce, cruel toward every human weakness, contemptuous of the poor, chauvinistic to the point of hysteria. We forget that the first constitutional separation of church and state was meant to safeguard *religion* as well as religious freedom. Emerson, Whitman, Melville, Dickinson, and Faulkner, along with Dostoevsky, Kafka, and Camus, would have said that not having enough to think about beyond *our* health, *our* sex life, *our* status, we are not thinking at all. Milosz is important not because he lectures us on the European agony we did not experience, but because of the example he sets as poet and teacher. Poetry to him is profoundly a recall, not a mere presentation of lived experience. It resembles what he calls "the cries of Job," not our endless defenses and explorations of the ego. Everything depends on what is left of faith after credulity has vanished from our practical, issue-tormented lives. It is important, essential, to restore the fundamental recognition that the world remains as strange to us as it ever was.

Years ago, when I discovered Milosz, I made a particular note of his saying, "Nothing could stifle my inner certainty that a shining point exists where all lines intersect." Inner certainty, an incredible gift. But I think what Milosz was in certainty about, first of all, was that "shining point."

Inner certainty is not the self-confidence that writers are supposed to feel when they sit down to write. It is not what Thoreau had in mind when he boasted, "You have to be strong in the legs to write." If there is a writer who is not filled with fear and trembling as he begins and begins and begins, he has to be an amateur. After publishing a score of books, Van Wyck Brooks said, "I feel every morning that I am on trial for my life and will not be acquitted."

Inner certainty is the hope and prayer, the absolute strangeness of believing, even in so destructive and fanatical an age as ours, that one's writing is important. The Polish poet in a burning city could not be sure that anyone would survive to read him, but he wrote anyway. Morally and imaginatively, he could not live without the connections writing makes, without believing in his heart that somehow, somewhere, despite the cruel wisdom of the age that nothing is less probable or perhaps less desirable, all lines do intersect. Milosz could never be sure, but somehow his work survived, to be read not only in Polish but in English decades later.

This kind of writer goes against the grain of those

who now deride E. M. Forster's "Only connect!" as old-fashioned, too simple, too wistful. These ideologues ignore the imponderables of existence that are still with us after all the work of science, technology, analytic philosophy, psychology, deconstruction, or linguistics, after all the political, racial, and sexual debate so hot in the academy. For the ideologues, there is no other world except the one right in front of their eyes. And in this world nothing lasts; books are as perishable as magazines, advertisements, movies, or television; and the academy is so preoccupied with status that it can proclaim literature to be only a branch of criticism, just another "discourse."

Yet, as Gertrude Stein said, remarks are not literature. Literature is not theory but, at best, the value we can give to our experience, which in our century has been and remains beyond the imagination of mankind. Of course not everyone has had the same experience. There are participants and there are bystanders. In the beginning was the deed and, since a deed has consequences, in the end is the deed. It is because there is no end to consequences that all lines finally intersect. But where—how—is the writer to be found who will have the inner certainty to see our life with the eyes of faith, and so make the world shine again?